VENUS

VENUS

Hanif Kureishi

faber and faber

First published in 2006
by Faber and Faber Limited
3 Queen Square, London WCIN 3AU

Typeset by Country Setting, Kingsdown, Kent CT14 8ES
Printed in England by Mackays of Chatham plc, Chatham, Kent

Hanif Kureishi is hereby identified as author of this work
in accordance with Section 77 of the Copyright, Designs
and Patents Act 1988

A CIP record for this book
is available from the British Library

ISBN 978–0571–23589–6
0–571–23589–1

2 4 6 8 10 9 7 5 3 1

CONTENTS

MAD OLD MEN

The Writing of *Venus*

Sometimes, if I am writing, and things are not going well, or if I am just bored, I will stop to read, until I want to write again. It is rare that I will read much fiction; the last thing a writer needs is another insistent writer's voice in his head. So these days I read only on trains or planes, where I can get dreamy with a book away from others, and with nothing else to do, and no other obligations. Also, it is an increasingly rare pleasure to discover a writer one has hardly heard of before, a writer one instantly likes and wants to read more of, a writer who speaks to you.

It was on a long train journey that I first read Tanizaki's novel, *Diary of a Mad Old Man*. It had been sent to me by an American friend who knew I'd just read Tanizaki's *The Key*. I had been told it was his best book, but I was keen to read other works. Tanizaki's name might not mean a lot even to well-informed readers – he was a huge influence on Mishima – but his books have remained in print in most European languages.

Diary of a Mad Old Man, a novella, is the story of a dying man and his son's wife, with whom he becomes infatuated, even as she treats him cruelly – and violently – at times. Other parts of the novel concern the kabuki theatre and the actors who work in it. It is not only a good novel: had it just been that, I could have read it and put it down. But as I began to read, there was a surge of recognition: I had been seeking this for a while. In the three years since the last film Roger Michel directed from my work, *The Mother*, I had been considering a similar idea to Tanizaki's, one I hadn't been ready to write, not knowing how to approach it. The difficulty of beginning a new piece of work is often the difficulty of finding a point a view, a way into the story, a place to start.

I read *Diary of a Mad Old Man* quickly and didn't read it again. It was not my intention to adapt the novel for film. This had already been done, and it seemed pointless to try to squash a work successful in one form into another. I would have to start again. But there was a lot in the story which appealed to me. Unlike Tanizaki, though, I was interested in another subject I believed I could use too: friendship between older men. One way to engage with another writer, to get closer to him than by mere reading, is to 'write around' his ideas, to develop them in your own register until the original becomes almost unrecognisable.

On most Fridays for years I have been having breakfast with a group of friends in Notting Hill. Occasionally, we would persuade a couple of younger women to join us. Mostly, nevertheless, it was only older men – actors, writers, theatre and film directors – people I'd known since I first began to work in London, in the mid-seventies. One morning we were talking about sleep and how to induce it, a popular and important subject amongst the over-forties. We discussed sleeping pills and sleeping draughts, and then about how to overcome the inevitable addiction. One of my friends and I would then shuffle off to the chemist, where he would get his pills. This friend said he found our Friday mornings to be particularly relaxing, compared to the difficulty of the rest of his life. He suggested he'd be happy sitting in a coffee shop, like old men he'd seen in Cairo, discussing world affairs while drinking tea and smoking a hookah.

It seems like a good idea; but how satisfying would it really be? In his long autobiographical essay 'In Praise of Shadows', Tanizaki movingly tells us how he built his house. He speaks of a kind of Zen attentiveness; he wants to praise age, slowness, wandering, curiosity, and the infinite pleasures of aesthetic appreciation. As in his fiction, baths and toilets are never far from his thoughts. Tanizaki tells us he likes to listen to the 'softly falling rain' while sitting on the toilet.

It is an admirable essay in many ways, reminding us of the virtues of silence and of listening; of space, emptiness and patience. Interestingly, Tanizaki's attitude towards the West at that time is not unlike that of some of the Muslim world today. The West represents the dangerous new: tradition and stability is being destroyed by an inferno of consumerism and post-modern sexuality. Tanizaki speaks of suffering 'a severe nervous disorder'.

The attitudes expressed in the essay sit uneasily with the rest of his work; indeed, they seem to be at odds with it. To a certain extent this illustrates the falsity, or impossibility perhaps, of an autobiography, of the belief that one can say, 'I am speaking the truth,' and be sure that that is what one is doing. This assumes that 'the truth' resides in what one knows, rather than in that which one doesn't. It might have to be admitted, then, that the 'truth' of an artist is more likely to be discovered in their fiction than in direct witness. In his 'lies', and in the relation between the characters, Tanizaki seems to get closer to the way things seem. Not only do his people not know anything about themselves for certain, they certainly don't know who they will become; the more they try to control themselves, the more out of hand everything becomes. It is not insignificant that, after writing screenplays and directing a movie, Tanizaki translated into Japanese Wilde's *The Picture of Dorian Gray* – the story of a sexually obsessed man who is unable to remain true to the image he has of himself.

By the time he wrote *The Key*, Tanizaki's work had been stripped down to the essentials of human interaction. He wrote: 'Western writers are overrich in their production. The offerings of writers like Zola and Balzac are like a feast within a feast. Just looking at the menu is enough to make us melancholy and get our laxatives ready.'

The Key concerns a middle-aged, ordinary couple with an adult daughter who still lives with them. From the ruins of what appears to be a long dead marriage, something starts to stir. We like to believe – it is a common misconception – that erotic relationships only deteriorate, that there is nothing new that can happen between a long-established couple. This is something we are so certain of that it must be incorrect. A deep involvement may become so distressingly pleasurable that we might feel dangerously addicted. As such a relationship develops, distance might be required, as the relationship begins to feel dangerous, even incestuous.

The novel opens with a middle-aged man drugging his sexually cold wife in order to spend more time with her feet. The sexuality of both of them is in the process of being re-aroused by the constant presence in their house of their daughter's fiancé. Here jealousy makes passion possible. As Lacan puts it, 'The other holds the key to the object desired.' Tanizaki doesn't bother with social detail but provides only the most necessary information about the city and the characters' social circumstances. And despite the fact that his characters are always medicating themselves – they are often sick, or imagine they are; no one is ever allowed to forget their body – his novels are frantic. In *The Key*, and in *Diary of a Mad Old Man*,

ix

the male and female characters, of whatever age, are too passionately involved with one another's desire – and the satisfaction, humiliation and family complications which follow from it – to settle for the seemingly nirvanic existence their circumstances might allow.

The couple begin drinking heavily; she becomes more westernised. A formerly modest woman, she repeats, with her husband, the ways of love-making she has just practised with her lover, whom she meets in the afternoons. When she then calls out the name of this other man – the man who will, at the end of the book, marry her daughter – the husband writes in his diary, 'At last, as her voice was rising once again, I took her. At that moment I felt I had burst into another world. This was reality, the past was only an illusion. Perhaps it would kill me, but this moment would last for ever.' His wish is granted. In the end, he dies, or is killed, perhaps by the effort involved, while making love to his wife.

Desire is the devil in Tanizaki, a torment you can never escape or fulfil, except temporarily. Yet without it there is inertia, emptiness, routine. On top of this, particularly as people age and there is less novelty available to them, desire is only sustained by others; by jealousy, rivalry, secrecy and human obstacles. Relief is only ever a reprieve, and the characters are forced towards extinction by their never-ending desire. Tanizaki is not an experimental writer himself; he is a straightforward writer, not a modernist. But his characters' lives become experimental once they engage with what they really want, once they realise they cannot escape their sexuality. Self-knowledge is impossible, foolish even, and wisdom a waste of time. All you can do is try to follow your body.

Feet are important to Tanizaki but there is something else too. Perverse objects are invested with symbolic magic. The fetish, not unlike Winnicott's 'transitional object', enables the child to pass from the mother to the world, carrying a piece of her. It could be anything: shoes, an item of underwear, hair, leather, silk, depending on where in his life the subject became fascinated by something he desired but was unable to understand. Freud even quotes the example of a man who fetishes 'the shine on someone's nose'. Couldn't a fetish be a book? Presumably this wouldn't be unusual in a writer.

In the end, as it would have to be, we discover that the key to *The Key* is writing – the human desire to make an authentic mark. Whether it be a cave drawing, scratching one's name on a cell wall, writing a novel, or cutting one's arm, all are communications, addressed to someone else, whether or not they exist in reality. *The Key* is constructed from diaries; the entire adventure is sustained by the erotics of secret writing and the fact that none of the characters can be sure whether the other is reading their diary at all. They can only hope – and fear – that they are. It is only here, in the intimate confessional of their words, in the truth of their unconscious, as it were, that one may come to know the other.

What is amazing to me is how a writer like Tanizaki can still speak to us. Before, let's say, the mid-seventies, when the Murdoch press began in earnest in Britain, it seemed there were areas of privacy into which no one but the novelist could venture. A novel didn't have to be sexually explicit to lay bare and obvious the intricacies of subjective private life. It did this fictionally and metaphorically. These were made-up stories, but we knew they represented real people in their deepest selves. But the 'real' itself was protected, it was behind the veil. Now, it seems, we know everything because nothing is hidden. I feel I would recognise Bill Clinton's penis in a crowd of other penises.

Yet a novel like *The Key* can still resonate and seem aggressively contemporary, making our desire seem as strange, and even alien – surely the point of literature – as it was before the age of explicitness. What is the truth about sexuality? Is sex pornography, prostitution or perversion? Is it being blown by a stranger in a toilet? Is it being tied up or is it fantasy? Or is it really full genital sex with one's spouse while thinking of no one else? Tanizaki shows us that sex is everywhere, and it involves not only transgression, but punishment, too, and suffering; it is a dirty business and probably has to be.

Tanizaki's work reminds me in some ways of the photographer Araki's work. (There is a photograph by Araki which leads me to Tanizaki. It is a nude in black gloves and stockings, with a key suspended from a band around her throat.) Araki has never taken an ugly picture; he is a photographer who, given time, would photograph the whole world. His pictures are a diary of his numerous interests. He is, obviously, more explicit in every way than Tanizaki, and perhaps more perverse. (In Tanizaki the women speak, act and deny; in Araki they are only ever objects.) But Araki is very good at picking up on the sexuality of the ordinary. He can photograph flowers, fruit, street scenes, and see the sexuality in them. Is this the extremity of perversion, or is it love for the world?

In Tanizaki's earlier novel *Naomi*, the male protagonist, much older than his lover, who becomes a convert to the pleasures of group sex, states, 'I started a diary in which I recorded everything about Naomi that caught my attention.' Naomi herself becomes almost a prostitute, except that, subversively, she refuses to be paid for the pleasure she receives and gives.

Written four years after *The Key*, *Diary of a Mad Old Man* is, of course, another diary. 'Even if you're impotent you have a kind of sex life,' writes the seventy-four-year-old protagonist, somewhat optimistically. Unfortunately, he has false teeth, and, looking at himself, states, 'Not even monkeys have such hideous faces. How could anyone with a face like this appeal to a woman?'

But he does appeal to her – in some way – though Tanizaki doesn't give us her point of view. And she appeals to him. This woman, his son's wife, Satsuko, is spiteful, sarcastic, a bit of a liar, a little power-crazed. Even so, he begins to love her, horribly so. With some encouragement from her, he tries to peep at her in the shower. When she slaps him, he buys her jewellery. In return she lets him kiss her feet and suck her toes. She forbids him to kiss her – making it clear she finds him disgusting – but at one point she lets drop a little saliva into his mouth.

His deterioration, the story of a man becoming aware of his imminent death, takes up as much space as this intriguing love making. There is also more than enough about pills, painkillers and suppositories. (Physical illness and decline serves, perhaps, as a metaphor for sexual corruption.) Then, in a delirium, he recalls a recent dream about his mother, a beautiful woman who smokes a pipe and whose feet, like those of Satsuko, he admires. 'Mother's feet were fairly broad, like those of the Bodhisattva of Mercy.' His mother, he knows, would be appalled by him 'petting' with his son's wife, 'even sacrificing his wife and children to try to win her love,' as he puts it.

When, for a short time, the old man's health improves, he requests to be taken on a trip to Kyoto. He wants to see the city for the last time, and to find a burial place. He also wants to have his headstone carved. He will have the imprints of Satsuko's feet – which he will take himself – carved into his headstone, along with an image of the Bodhisattva of Mercy. The women he loves, mother and 'lover' combined, will be walking on him throughout eternity.

It seems scandalous, humorously dishonest even, for an old man to prefer a young woman's feet to his own wife, or to anyone in his family. Yet Tanizaki appears to be saying that even at the very end of a life the self doesn't only want to survive. The *Diary* shows, at least, the persistence of desire; it is, perhaps, a tribute to its strength. But there is no doubt that it is a fetishistic relationship, and could be described as infatuation, not as love. This might have been intriguing had Tanizaki provided more idea of what Satsuko wants from the old man, apart from his fascination. He seems to suggest that she is only materialistic, and manipulative; anyhow, the relationship doesn't alter much as it goes on.

Tanizaki's *Diary of a Mad Old Man* provokes more questions than it seems to answer, which is part of its intelligence. How little guilt the protagonist feels, and no embarrassment, over his attachment to Satsuko's feet! He seems so at ease with his fetish that we cannot forfeit the impression that he has pursued it before. But Tanizaki fails to tell us the place of such preoccupations in the old man's life, whether this is a late outbreak – a final burst, as it were – or whether his fetishism has been his life's work. If you were adapting the novel for film these are questions you'd not only have to ask, but to decide on.

In 1927, around the time he was thinking about religion and society, Freud wrote an essay, 'Fetishism', in which he mentions the Chinese custom of mutilating the female foot, and of worshipping it when it has been mutilated. He says, 'It seems as though the Chinese male wants to thank the woman for having submitted to being castrated.' Tanizaki became interested in Freud as a student and the Complete Works were translated and published in Japan between 1929 and 1933. Also in this paper, Freud tells us that the fetish is a substitute for the penis, being an 'approach to the genitals from below'. But not any penis. Here Freud makes a bold, new move: he tells us that the fetish stands for the missing penis of the woman; of, in fact, the mother. All fetishists, according to Freud, have an aversion to the actual genitals, for which the object is a substitute. Not that this is unusual. Freud makes a further startling statement here, 'Probably no male human being is spared the fright of castration at the sight of a female genital.' (Freud suggests that it is enough to make anyone homosexual.)

If an old man sucks on a younger woman's toes, is he, at this moment, regressing also to childhood? Oddly, and perhaps wisely – showing his subtlety as a writer – Tanizaki doesn't comment on the old man's obsession: he merely shows it. Tanizaki is a psychologist in the sense that he is spellbound by his character's internal lives, of that which is offered only symbolically to the world. But he'd never be so crude as to tie a whole aspect of experience to one cause. By not being over-insistent or too schematic, Tanizaki leaves us with more symbolic complexities. The work of an imaginative writer is to suggest, not to solve.

Yet without doubt there is something of an enigma in the book here. The old man himself, an intelligent, cultured man, has no curiosity about his own preferences. It seems unlikely, but he never questions this sudden enthralment. This is not so unusual: Freud asserts that few people seek analysis because of a fetish. Most go because they have difficulties at work; the fetish might not be mentioned for a long time, if at all. Not that fetishistic pleasure would be that unusual. For Freud, the child is the ultimate narcissist and pervert, concerned only with his own pleasure and, perhaps, how to stage and re-stage it. Others are merely actors in this scenario. Perhaps sexual feeling is so powerful it has to be modified, by an obstacle, in order to be bearable.

In his own way Tanizaki does take these ideas further, throwing open the whole question of love itself, of what it is we love about the other. The characters in his work are deeply involved with others. But in what way and what does it mean? How do perversion and love interact? Is fetish love real love? Is being excited by only a part of the other real sex? Is fetishism a version of love, or its obverse? Is it only, as Havelock Ellis designated it, 'auto-erotic'?

Much as they might like to be, Tanizaki's characters cannot be self-sufficient. They never stop needing one another, or trying to solidify that need. As both characters struggle for ultimate, complete control over the other, the engagement is almost comical. Tanizaki is aware that in the end you are always dependent on the other; indeed, you are, partly, creating them, having them play a role with which you identify. This is not only the case in exhibitionism or voyeurism, but in sadism too. Yet the freedom of the other, which resides in their words – or perhaps a diary – will ultimately elude you; it has to. Total control would end in the death or murder of one of the subjects, at which point the game ends.

The novel left me with a strong after-impression, and the sense that the film I wanted to write would be concerned with some of these ideas. After I'd made some notes and sketched out several scenes, the director, Roger Michel, and I, began to assemble the elements of the film, which would concern two elderly actors and a girl who comes to stay with one of them.

It wasn't long before *Venus* began to move away from the Tanizaki set-up. The relationship had to be less claustrophobic and more complex, always dipping and turning. If the man wants something from the girl, she wants something else from him, so that their relationship becomes a series of successful misunderstandings. Failed exchanges are, at least, a kind of exchange. *Venus* also concerns a girl finding a father; at the end, briefly, she finds a mother too. Then she can leave home again.

It is the girl who makes the story work. Her entry onto the scene disturbs all their lives. But why a girl? Even political correctness always leaves someone – or a group – out; it needs to. A new scapegoat is created. I noticed that young working-class women – slags, mingers, munters, dogs, chavs – were easy targets, perfectly representing our greed, lasciviousness, immorality. Condemned for the pursuit of pleasure, and regarded only as consumers without inner texture, they are one of the few groups who can be satirised without complaint, damned for their stupidity and inarticulacy; a group with no lobbyists and little power. It is a new snobbery, and almost unnoticed. Why not develop such a character, and, combining them with the conventional idea of a stranger coming to stay, see where it goes?

I couldn't move forward with the film until I saw how it might end. I tried numerous exits. Perhaps I didn't want to accept it could only end one way. It was Roger who saw it had to finish with a journey and a death. As a child my family would go on holiday to the Kent resorts, and I'd started taking my children to Whitstable with its beach huts and stony beach. For a while I'd been thinking of setting a story there. Of course, both *The Key* and the *Diary* end with the death of the male protagonist; and it is, in fact, illness which precipitates them into late desire. How else, then, could the novel end? It is only death which gives life true intensity.

Venus

CAST AND CREW

Venus received its world premiere
at the Toronto Film Festival in September 2006

PRINCIPAL CAST

MAURICE	Peter O'Toole
IAN	Leslie Phillips
VENUS	Jodie Whittaker
VALERIE	Vanessa Redgrave
DONALD	Richard Griffiths

PRINCIPAL CREW

Directed by	Roger Michell
Screenplay by	Hanif Kureishi
Produced by	Kevin Loader
Executive Producers	Tessa Ross
	Scott Rudin
	Miles Ketley
	Charles Moore
Line Producer	Rosa Romero
Cinematography	Haris Zambarloukos
Film Editing	Nicolas Gaster
Production Design	John-Paul Kelly
Costume Design	Natalie Ward
Hair and Make-Up Design	Daniel Phillips
Music	Corinne Bailey Rae
Casting	Fiona Weir

EXT. THE SEA. DAY

The grey sea: featureless, endless.

INT. MAURICE'S BEDROOM. DAWN.

An old man, Maurice, sits on the edge of his bed, staring into the distance.

INT. DOCTOR'S SURGERY WAITING ROOM. DAY

Maurice sits in a busy doctor's waiting room. Kids run around; people of all ages and types mill about. Christmas carols play in the background and there is a sad-looking nativity scene. There is a window through which you talk to the receptionist. Someone is having an argument.

PERSON
But I need to see him now! I'm sick – I can't bleedin' wait!

INT. DOCTOR'S SURGERY. DAY

A Doctor squirts lubricant onto his finger.

DOCTOR
Going anywhere nice for the holidays?

Maurice mumbles.

Where?

MAURICE
(*almost incomprehensible*)
Piranha fish.

The rubber finger approaches his arse.

DOCTOR
Fantastic . . . I've been there. Ah-ha . . .

The rubber index finger goes into his arse and the Doctor moves it around and from side to side, exploring.

There we go, easy but not necessarily nice.

Maurice groans.

Uncomfortable, eh? That's normal. I'd feel the same. Everything all right otherwise? Life treating you well?

Maurice makes another noise.

Good . . . good.

There's a silence before the finger comes out. The doctor removes the glove and throws it into the bin.

INT. DOCTOR'S SURGERY. DAY

Later. Maurice sits opposite the doctor again.

DOCTOR
The prostate should feel like a peach – with a groove down the centre. Yours is a little bumpy – there might be a small nodule there, but it could easily be nothing – so we need to send you to a specialist. A lot of older men have this problem. It rarely kills them.

MAURICE
They die of something else first?

DOCTOR
Right. So you should worry a little but not a lot. Now then.

He starts typing into his computer.

INT. DOCTOR'S SURGERY NURSE'S ROOM. DAY

He's in another room at the doctor's. A Nurse takes blood. He watches. Meanwhile Nurse One talks to Nurse Two, who is in the doorway.

NURSE TWO
I said I didn't mind what she did . . . but there's no way I'm sharing a tent with her after last year – I've made that clear.

NURSE ONE

Good on yer –

NURSE TWO

In the end there was such a stream of – you know –

NURSE ONE

Yes, exactly –

NURSE TWO

Coming and going and all that, that I felt like standing outside and shouting: another warm body for my friend!

NURSE ONE

You should have. (*To Maurice.*) That's fine. All done. (*Looking at him for the first time.*) Are you all right?

MAURICE

Yes, I'm fine, thanks.

EXT. STREET. DAY

Maurice is walking along.

INT. CAFÉ. DAY

Maurice is finishing breakfast with Ian, who drinks tea.

IAN

Why were you late?

MAURICE

I overslept.

IAN

You actually slept?

MAURICE

Yes. I consider any kind of sleep to be a triumph.

IAN

Indeed. Now. Shall we?

MAURICE

We shall.

They go through their pockets putting pill bottles on the table in front of them, opening them up and gobbling the contents.

IAN

What have I got today? You should try these. You'll never wake up.

MAURICE

It's the waking-up pills I'm looking for now.

IAN

Anything blue I'd recommend for that.

MAURICE

White ones give me more of a thrill.

Ian reads the side of the pill box.

IAN

'Do not operate heavy machinery. Keep away from children.'

MAURICE

Biblical advice.

The Waitress puts down their bill.

WAITRESS

There you are, gentlemen.

MAURICE

Excellent, my dear.

As she goes he admires her legs, somewhat wearily.

IAN

Have you got my glasses?

MAURICE

No, you've got them.

IAN

Why would I have them? I'm not wearing them, am I? Christ, I've lost them now – that's the worst thing that's ever happened –

MAURICE

They're in your right hand.

IAN

Oh yes.

MAURICE

You wouldn't survive five minutes without me.

IAN

But I'm getting help.

MAURICE

You're not? Professional?

IAN

My niece's girl.

MAURICE

What niece? You kept your family well hidden until now. Not with good reason, I hope. They must be either terribly beautiful or terribly ugly. (*Pause.*) You won't like it, Ian, another human presence in the vicinity.

IAN

Come on. We're off.

MAURICE

Where to?

IAN

Shopping.

INT. HABERDASHERS SHOP. DAY

The two men are examining pink sheets.

IAN

I think the very very pink as opposed to the quite pink, don't you?

MAURICE

Have you worked out what the girl will actually do?

IAN

She'll shop and cook for me. In exchange she can stay in the flat for a few weeks, while she looks for a job.

MAURICE

A sort of nurse, then.

IAN

Only cheaper. (*Looks at Maurice.*) No uniform. Don't give yourself a coronary.

MAURICE

Will she bathe you?

IAN

Daily. Do you think they sell loofahs?

EXT. STREET MARKET. DAY

Ian inspects some grapefruit, holding them like tits, closing his eyes.

MAURICE
(*rolling his eyes*)
How well do you remember this girl?

IAN

Well enough. But I might be confusing her with her sister.

MAURICE

Really?

IAN

Whoever she is, she's definitely my own flesh and blood. Envious, eh?

MAURICE

Enormously.

EXT. STREET. DAY

They walk along together.

IAN

At the hospital they said if I'm clear in five years I'm safe. I said by then I'll be drinking with Jesus.

MAURICE

He's looking forward to meeting you. He loved your
Polonius. But he found your Caesar a little weak.

IAN

Weak?

MAURICE

A little . . .

IAN

What?

MAURICE

Fruity.

IAN

No he fucking didn't. Did he? Fruity? What the fuck!
Fruity!

Maurice laughing.

Fucking fruit . . .

INT. IAN'S FLAT. DAY

Maurice heaves Ian's bags on the table.

MAURICE

I'm parched. How about a little drinkie?

IAN

This isn't a pub. I've got to get her room ready.

Maurice follows Ian into the spare room.

MAURICE

Can I help?

INT. IAN'S FLAT SPARE BEDROOM. DAY

Maurice attempts to help Ian make up the bed with the pink sheets.

IAN

Don't flap it about like that, Maurice, I'm getting wind rash.

                         MAURICE
      Let me tuck it in, you'll tire yourself.

Maurice tucks in the sheets. Ian watches him.

                           IAN
      She'll suffocate in there.

                         MAURICE
      There's no reason for her to move around unnecessarily at
      night.

                           IAN
      Not unless she needs to attend to me.

                         MAURICE
      In what way?

                           IAN
      I've put a little bell by my bed. If I feel unwell I can tinkle it.

                         MAURICE
      I bet she can't wait to hear that little tinkle.

                           IAN
      Martha says she's one of the the most compassionate
      people in the Greater Manchester area.

INT. IAN'S FLAT BATHROOM. DAY

Ian shows Maurice the towel he's bought.

                           IAN
      I've bought her a pink towel too so there's no confusion in
      the bathroom.

                         MAURICE
      No, you wouldn't want that.

INT. IAN'S FLAT KITCHEN. DAY

                           IAN
      And in case she wants something to read I've got her these.

Ian holds up a Borders bag: there are several volumes: Zola's Nana, *Turgenev's* First Love, *Larkin's* Poems, *and Wharton's* Age of Innocence.

MAURICE

No one likes Wharton.

IAN

I really want to educate the girl, Maurice. To pass something on.

MAURICE

Yes, dear.

IAN

Anyway, Martha says the girl reads in her room for hours on end and she loves music. While we're eating tonight I thought we could listen to the St Matthew Passion.

He holds up a brand new boxed set of Bach CDs.

MAURICE

Lovely.

IAN

No doubt it'll be tomato soup and a Temazepam for you.

MAURICE

No doubt.

IAN

Why don't you ring Valerie if you feel lonely?

MAURICE

When is this nurse person actually arriving?

IAN

In an hour or so. What do you think? Shall I get her to run me a nice bath and put my dressing gown on the radiator? I hope she can do a rocket salad. Or something interesting with fish.

EXT. IAN'S FLAT STAIRS. DAY

Maurice leaves, mumbling to himself.

> MAURICE
> Something interesting with fish . . .

EXT. STREET. DAY

Maurice walks home.

INT. MAURICE'S FLAT. DAY

Maurice is on the phone.

> MAURICE
> Yes, yes, I do . . . I'm too tired to come in. Give it to me
> straight. I can take it. (*Pause.*) Oh God. What sort of
> operation? When? Hold on – let me sit down.

INT. ART ROOM. DAY

*Maurice is in his drawing class, holding his pencil. The model is a
middle-aged woman. He contemplates her body. When the Teacher
walks behind him, to look at his work, we see that Maurice has drawn
nothing. He stares into the middle distance. The Teacher looks at him
sympathetically.*

> TEACHER
> Everything okay here?

INT. MAURICE'S FLAT BEDROOM. DAY

*He sits on his bed, exhausted and disheartened. Slaps himself on the
side of the face.*

> MAURICE
> Come on, old man.

INT. MAURICE'S FLAT BEDROOM. DAY

*Maurice, more cheerful now, is taking his trousers out of his wardrobe.
We see other trousers on the bed, which he has been trying on.*

INT. MAURICE'S FLAT. DAY

Maurice is looking at himself in the mirror, flattening his hair etc.

                    MAURICE
              (*in his actor's deep voice*)
Me, me, me, me, me – her, her, her—him, him, him, him –

EXT. STREET. DAY

Maurice walks jauntily along.

EXT./INT. IAN'S FLAT HALLWAY. DAY

Ian opens the door.

                    IAN
                (*sotto voce*)
Help me! Help me!

                    MAURICE
What on earth –?

                    IAN
Thank Christ you're here.

                    MAURICE
What's up?

INT. IAN'S LIVING ROOM. DAY

                    IAN
I can't begin to tell you. She's –

                    MAURICE
What?

                    IAN
Oh, horrible, horrible . . . foul and vile beyond belief!

                    MAURICE
What is it? Was the bath too cool or the towel too hot? Was
the fish overcooked?

IAN

Fish? I'd have been lucky to get a fish finger inserted into my rectum.

MAURICE

What's gone wrong?

IAN

Oh God, Maurice, it's hardly been twenty-four hours and already I'm screaming for euthanasia.

Without warning Jessie comes out of another room. She is not pretty; she is plain. Maurice stares at her. She disappears into the kitchen.

MAURICE

What is she doing in there?

IAN

Who cares? Don't go in, whatever you do.

MAURICE

Shouldn't you be getting ready?

IAN

For what?

MAURICE

The theatre.

IAN

Thank God. Let's leave immediately. I'll just change. Marvellous. Let's hope it's a long play.

MAURICE

You've never said that before.

Ian goes into his bedroom.

Maurice considers for a moment and then wanders over and pokes his head into the kitchen. She is sitting there eating a bag of crisps.

I'm Maurice. Maurice. You?

She says nothing.

Can I?

Maurice starts to find himself a glass and a bottle and pours himself a drink.

> You will find that I usually come over around this time,
> for a little drinky. I like whisky with a whisker of water.
> No more than a whisker, though. That ruins it. It's called
> 'drowning'. Drowning. Do you know how to mix drinks?
> No? Once acquired, it's a talent that will serve you for life.
> Like . . . typing.

Jessie looks at him for a moment and then goes into the living room.

INT. IAN'S LIVING ROOM. DAY

Maurice follows her out into the living room with his drink. Jessie is sitting in Ian's chair eating the crisps and watching a soap.

MAURICE

So. What are you doing? In London, I mean.

JESSIE

Looking for work.

MAURICE

What sort of work?

JESSIE

Work. You know. Work.

MAURICE

Yes, yes, I know all about it. Any particular kind?

JESSIE

Modelling.

MAURICE

There can't be much call for that.

JESSIE

Call for what?

MAURICE

Yodelling.

JESSIE

Not yodelling. Yodelling! Modelling. You know. (*She makes a gesture.*) You know anyone in the modelling field?

MAURICE

Yes. I know everyone. Do you have a fall-back position?

JESSIE

No. (*She eats a crisp.*) No. I don't need one.

MAURICE

Right.

JESSIE

You saying I do?

MAURICE

No. I wouldn't say that. No.

JESSIE

No. Good.

MAURICE

I was in a commercial, years ago. For Camel cigarettes.

JESSIE

Have you got any on you?

MAURICE

I can get you some.

JESSIE

Really?

MAURICE

Oh yes. They're delicious. There's no better way to die.

JESSIE

I'm thirsty now. Could I have a beer? I told him to get some in.

MAURICE

What did he say?

JESSIE

He said it was a slippery slope.

MAURICE

He did? You better have one right away.

JESSIE

In the bottle, please.

MAURICE

Right-oh.

INT. IAN'S FLAT KITCHEN. DAY

Maurice searches for beers in the kitchen: in the cupboards, fridge etc. In the end he finds them in the oven.

MAURICE

Why's he put them in there?

JESSIE

He's stupid.

MAURICE

Not that stupid.

He turns and sees that she is standing in the doorway.

Oh.

He opens the beer and hands it to her. She puts it against her face, to test its coolness.

JESSIE

A cup of tea would have been colder.

MAURICE

I'll take it –

JESSIE

No.

He watches her drink. Maurice feels a little uncomfortable.

MAURICE

Ian – Where is he? Could you – Would you mind going to see how far he's got?

JESSIE

I don't like to go into a man's bedroom.

MAURICE

Of course not.

INT. IAN'S FLAT BEDROOM. DUSK

*Maurice goes into the bedroom and finds Ian asleep on the bed,
having failed to get changed. Maurice picks up the little bell by the
bed. He's tempted to tinkle it, but puts it back. Then he pulls a cover
over Ian.*

INT. IAN'S FLAT KITCHEN. DUSK

Jessie is eating. Maurice holds the theatre tickets.

MAURICE

Oh come on. What will you do otherwise?

JESSIE

Watch telly.

MAURICE

It won't be as good as *Celebrity Love Island*. But it'll be live.

JESSIE

Live?

MAURICE

You might enjoy it.

JESSIE

I'll have to get changed.

MAURICE

I'd like that.

JESSIE

The theatre's posh, isn't it?

MAURICE

We'll be in the cheap seats.

She goes.

Where we belong.

INT. IAN'S FLAT HALLWAY. NIGHT

A bit later. Maurice is hovering around Jessie's door. She is playing quite loud Missy Elliott music. Maurice looks at his watch.

                    MAURICE
Jessie, we'd better –

                    JESSIE
                    (*calls out*)
Tell the taxi to wait.

                    MAURICE
Taxi? I've got my bus pass.

                    JESSIE
You'd better call one then.

                    MAURICE
                    (*uncertainly*)
Of course.

He goes to the telephone and puts on his glasses.

Er . . . do you have a number?

She comes out of the bedroom, having changed into a short skirt and heels. He stares at her.

                    JESSIE
All right?

                    MAURICE
Yes. Yes. Fine. Yes.

INT. TAXI. NIGHT

They're in a minicab. He watches her.

                    JESSIE
What are you looking at?

                    MAURICE
Nothing.

JESSIE

Why?

MAURICE

Why not?

EXT. SLOANE SQUARE. NIGHT

They get out of the taxi and Maurice pays the driver.

Jessie looks up at the theatre.

JESSIE

Can't we go and see *Billy Elliot*?

INT. ROYAL COURT THEATRE. NIGHT

Jessie is helping Maurice up the stairs to the Theatre Upstairs. It's really hard work for him, as well as for her.

MAURICE
(*tossing his head*)

I've worked here, you know.

JESSIE

You're sweating on me. I think it's gone in my mouth!

MAURICE

I'm sure you've swallowed worse.

JESSIE

I think I'm going to be sick!

INT. ROYAL COURT THEATRE UPSTAIRS. NIGHT

They go through the black curtain and into the theatre.

JESSIE

It's not very big.

MAURICE

That means we can see the acting.

JESSIE

Fuck.

INT. ROYAL COURT THEATRE UPSTAIRS. NIGHT

The play is set in a park. Three girls in their late teens, one with a pram.

GIRL
(*to Pram Girl*)

Come with us.

PRAM GIRL

I can't –

GIRL 3

It'll be a sick party.

PRAM GIRL

I just said I can't fucking come. I got this one here.

GIRL

Get a minder. Oh come on, you minger!

PRAM GIRL

Fuck off, just fuck off and fuck off and fuck off for ever!

GIRL

We know who the father is!

PRAM GIRL

Do yer?

GIRL 3

What a mess up you've made!

PRAM GIRL

Oh God no, no!

GIRL

Silly cow. You're in the biggest trouble of yer life!

They start to leave.

PRAM GIRL

Don't make me stand here on me own. I can't stand it. Now I've got no one!

Maurice looks at Jessie, who stares open-mouthed.

INT. ROYAL COURT FOYER BAR. NIGHT

Jessie and Maurice stand in the foyer with drinks. Behind him there's a photograph of Maurice with a more famous actor.

MAURICE

That was me.

JESSIE

You're famous.

MAURICE

A little bit.

JESSIE

What's your name again?

MAURICE

Maurice. Maurice Russell.

JESSIE

What have you been in?

MAURICE

Serjeant Musgrave's Dance – among many, many, many other things.

She shakes her head. The bell goes. The theatregoers begin to drift back to the theatre.

JESSIE

Isn't it the end?

MAURICE

It's never the end when you go to the theatre, I'm afraid.

Pause.

JESSIE

Say you had a turn.

MAURICE

What a good idea. I thought I could feel one coming on.

JESSIE

Come on.

They start to make their escape.

                    MAURICE
Are you taking me somewhere?

                    JESSIE
Yeah.

                    MAURICE
How wonderful.

INT. PUB. NIGHT

*She leads him into a pub crowded with young people; the music is
loud.*

                    JESSIE
I'll have a Bacardi Breezer.

                    MAURICE
Me too. What is it?

                    JESSIE
It's red.

                    MAURICE
Oh good. Like wine?

                    JESSIE
Is it?

INT. PUB. NIGHT

She drinks her drink. He looks at his and tastes it.

                    MAURICE
Unusual. A sort of cellophane effect. (*Beat.*) Are you
getting on well with your uncle?

                    JESSIE
Like a house on fire. Except . . .

                    MAURICE
What?

25

JESSIE

Do you know anything about fish?

MAURICE

Fuck all, my dear. You?

JESSIE

Fuck all.

MAURICE

You could consult a book.

JESSIE

A book?

MAURICE

Yes, you know, two flaps of card with printed paper in between.

JESSIE

Do you read a lot?

MAURICE

Only when there's no one to talk to.

Jessie drinks quickly, eyeing up the boys.

That went down a treat. Another?

He touches her arm. She stares at him with contempt.

JESSIE

I'll let you get me one more.

MAURICE

Thank you.

INT. PUB. NIGHT

He stands at the bar waving his twenty-pound note but he can't get served. He looks at her bouncing to the music.

EXT. SLOANE SQUARE. NIGHT

Jessie is quite drunk and Maurice is helping her along the street.

> JESSIE

We off somewhere nice?

> MAURICE

Jessie, you've got to help me . . .

> JESSIE

I am helping you!

> MAURICE

But you're bending to the left!

> JESSIE

You're pulling me!

It is difficult work for Maurice. He looks up and sees a cab in the distance.

> MAURICE

Got any money, my dear?

INT. TAXI. NIGHT

Jessie has more or less passed out. She crashes her head into his shoulder. He smells and sniffs at her neck and hair, even touching her face.

Maurice sees the Cabbie watching him in the mirror.

INT. IAN'S FLAT. NIGHT

As quietly as he can, Maurice helps her into the flat and finally drops her onto the sofa. He is creeping out when he hears Ian ringing the bell. Maurice giggles to himself. Then he trips over her outstretched leg and falls against a table. The lamp, pot plant, books, etc., crash over.

INT. HOSPITAL. DAY

Maurice is fighting for life on a hospital bed while numerous relatives ululate around him.

> MAURICE

Ahh! Ahh!

                              MAN
Dad, Dad! Don't leave us!

                              WOMAN
He's going!

                              MAN
Goodbye, goodbye –

                              GIRL
Goodbye, Dad!

                              DIRECTOR
Cut!

*The Director comes over, takes the other Actors away and begins to
talk to them. Maurice lies there forgotten, eyes closed. Then he looks at
his watch and takes a small cigar out of his pyjama pocket, sticking it
in his mouth. The Director comes over.*

Okay?

                              MAURICE
I think I am going to die.

Director laughs.

                              DIRECTOR
You can't die yet, Maurice, we haven't shot them carrying
the body out.

INT. 3-WAY TRAILER. DAY

*Maurice is sitting taking off his slap. Outside there is a table covered
with food for the actors. He picks up his stuff: keys, money. There is an
envelope of cash which the Runner gives him.*

                              RUNNER
There you are, Mr Russell, as requested.

                              MAURICE
Thanks, old chap. Can I take some of those cakes?

                              RUNNER
Sure, why not? I'll help you with them.

                               28

EXT. VALERIE'S HOUSE. NIGHT

This is a large old family house, in bad condition now. Maurice walks up the path holding the cakes in a box. Down the street some carol singers are knocking on doors.

INT. VALERIE'S HOUSE. NIGHT

Valerie is stationed with her cats. He sits beside her and she fans him with a newspaper.

> MAURICE
>
> I've been at it like a dog all day. I'm utterly broken.

> VALERIE
>
> What were you playing?

> MAURICE
>
> A corpse, more or less.

> VALERIE
>
> Type-cast again.

> MAURICE
>
> Here. I asked them for cash.

He gives her the money.

> VALERIE
>
> Not all of it.

> MAURICE
>
> Please, take it. Put it towards the boiler, it gets cold in here.

> VALERIE
>
> The whole thing's useless. It's got to be replaced, Maurice, the radiators and everything. The man came yesterday.

> MAURICE
>
> I owe you thousands. Over the years . . . you've been more than generous. I haven't forgotten.

> VALERIE
>
> No.

MAURICE

Can't the children contribute? Some of them even appear
to work for a living.

VALERIE

I'm ashamed, Maurice, that we can't look after ourselves at
our age.

INT. VALERIE'S HOUSE. NIGHT

*Maurice is standing on a chair trying to change a halogen light bulb.
Valerie is scoffing one of the cream cakes.*

VALERIE

I'm in such pain, dear, I don't want to live.

MAURICE

Yes you do. Almost all of us want to live. (*Pause.*) They say
I have to have an operation.

VALERIE

Oh Maurice. What is it?

MAURICE

Prostate. (*Pause.*) I'm sure it's just routine.

VALERIE

Oh Maurice, I'm so sorry.

MAURICE

You've always wanted to remove my balls surgically.

VALERIE

That's true. I just wish I could be there to see it. These
cakes are awfully nice.

INT. VALERIE'S HOUSE. NIGHT

Putting his coat on, he is about to go.

MAURICE

Valerie. Despite everything . . .

VALERIE

What?

MAURICE

Despite everything. My behaviour . . .

VALERIE

What is it, Maurice?

MAURICE

What I want to say is . . . I've always, always quite liked you.

VALERIE

No you haven't. I bore you.

MAURICE

Do you?

VALERIE

I bore myself.

MAURICE

Do you? Oh . . . oh . . . I am sorry . . .

VALERIE

Go home, Maurice.

MAURICE

Right-oh.

VALERIE

Oh, sorry. Oh stay – stay. I'll make up a bed for you in the study.

MAURICE

Spend the night with my wife? What are you thinking, my dear?

VALERIE

What a strange man you are, Maurice.

MAURICE

Yes, it's my only virtue.

INT. CAFÉ. DAY

Maurice and Donald sit there together looking at the papers. Suddenly Donald says:

DONALD

Sammy's gone.

MAURICE

He has? Christ.

DONALD

Big picture of him as a handsome young spunker.

MAURICE

Another one down.

DONALD

I did *Love's Labour's* with him in '71 . . . Northampton . . . no, no, York . . . I was lucky to get a single bloody line in without him chattering or moaning over it.

MAURICE

When he cried onstage it could break your heart. (*Beat.*) The *Othello*, do you remember?

DONALD

Peggy. Wasn't it?

MAURICE

Yes, yes, Peggy. (*Beat.*) I wonder how many lines I'll get.

DONALD

A paragraph. At least.

They see Ian approaching.

Here comes Caesar.

MAURICE

And moving rather rapidly for someone who's just picked up his disability cheque.

Ian hurries in and sits down.

DONALD

Hello, love.

IAN

Thank Christ, she's asleep now. She stays up late watching
TV and singing to herself. She's drunk all my best Stolly
as well as the Scotch. She's even put away the Drambuie
I was saving for your Christmas visit.

DONALD

God no –

IAN

I bought this lovely bit of halibut yesterday but she had no
idea what to do with it.

MAURICE

Jesus!

IAN

Her notion of cooking is to stick a plate of virtual sick into
the microwave. I asked her to clean the bathroom and she
said . . .

MAURICE

What?

IAN

Don't make me repeat it!

DONALD

Can't you call the police?

MAURICE

Yes. Good idea.

DONALD

Oh, just kill them, kill the young, exterminate their
disgusting happiness and hope!

IAN

It's not fucking funny. I've got high blood pressure. I could
die at any moment. (*Pause.*) If only I could find her a job I
could get rid of her.

MAURICE

Why can't she just go back home?

IAN

I rang my niece. I begged her. I wept more than Antigone.
I said I'd pay for a taxi to wherever. Martha says there are
no jobs in the countryside.

MAURICE

There must be some demand for barmaids and prostitutes.

DONALD

Exactly . . . Even in the country they need young women . . .
to lap dance.

IAN

What?

MAURICE

What would you know about that?

DONALD

You can learn a lot from television.

IAN

The fact is, Martha just doesn't want her back. The girl was
a barmaid. She got herself into some sort of trouble.

MAURICE

What sort of trouble?

Ian ignores him.

IAN

Well, they had to get the tart out of there. But to unleash
her on us like this . . .

DONALD

Maliciously –

MAURICE

Exactly.

IAN

It's pure evil . . .

DONALD

Of course it is. Did your niece do it deliberately?

34

IAN

Of course not. Are you saying my niece is a little cunt?

DONALD

Not a cunt, no.

IAN

What then? I'm at my wits' end and you men are laughing at me.

MAURICE

Yes, let's think about this, collectively.

IAN

Please . . . please, let's . . .

MAURICE

We hate you to suffer, Ian.

DONALD
(*to Maurice, indicating Ian*)
He's aged since she's been there.

IAN

No I haven't.

MAURICE

Yes, yes –

DONALD

Look at yourself.

IAN

You fucking look at yourself. Maurice, you're fond of women – all women, I know that – but I guarantee even you wouldn't last two days with her.

MAURICE

Pah!

IAN

Please, Maurice, you're not as sick as me, and you're resourceful, help me.

35

MAURICE

You couldn't have come to a better person. A scientist of the female heart.

DONALD

A professor of pussy –

IAN

Fucking shut it, Donald. You're really getting on my nerves.

MAURICE

Yes, shut it, Donald.

IAN
(to Maurice)
Thank you, friend. Thank you.

MAURICE

Isn't it your turn to pay for breakfast?

IAN

It might be, it might be.

Ian goes to pay.

DONALD
(to Maurice)
I'd take a photograph if I were you.

EXT. IAN'S FLAT. DAY

Maurice knocks on the door. Jessie opens it.

JESSIE

He's at the doctor's.

MAURICE

Good.

JESSIE

What?

He pushes past her.

INT. IAN'S FLAT KITCHEN. DAY

Jessie and Maurice sit at the kitchen table. She is eating a bacon buttie.

                    MAURICE
After scouring the earth on your behalf, Jessie, I'm here to announce I've got you a job.

                    JESSIE
Liar.

                    MAURICE
It's true. Modelling.

                    JESSIE
You've done that?

                    MAURICE
Yes. Pleased?

Jessie pushes away the sandwich.

I said you could rely on me.

                    JESSIE
What sort of clothes is it? D'you think they'll let me keep them at the end?

                    MAURICE
I'm not sure about that.

                    JESSIE
Why not?

                    MAURICE
There's no actual clothes involved.

                    JESSIE
What? None at all?

                    MAURICE
No. Not as such. No. No clothes. None at all.

                    JESSIE
You're having me do porno! I'm not letting anyone I know see my chuffs and bumps!

37

MAURICE

It's not like that.

JESSIE

What is it like then?

MAURICE

You'll see.

JESSIE

You better not be trying to corrupt me.

MAURICE

I am shocked, Jessie, that you would think of me like this.
I am a respectable and respected man.

JESSIE

Oh yeah, right.

MAURICE

Chuffs and bumps . . . I've never heard that before.

JESSIE

Now you're thinking about it.

MAURICE

I'm not – I promise!

JESSIE

You think about something else –

MAURICE

Okay – I am contemplating my own death. You can relax.

JESSIE

Jesus . . .

She picks up her sandwich.

When do I start?

INT. ART ROOM. EVENING

*Maurice and Jessie walk through the school towards the classroom.
He tries to take her arm.*

38

JESSIE

Don't keep touching me!

MAURICE

Suppose my legs go! I look young for my age, I know, but
I am a little weak.

JESSIE

That's no reason to cling on. Just let yourself fall to the
ground natural-like.

MAURICE

Thank you, my dear. (*He imitates her.*) 'Natural-like.'

INT. ART ROOM. EVENING

*Maurice sits in a circle with a group of other art students, his pad and
pencil in front of him, looking very cheerful.*

MAURICE

I think you'll all be very pleased.

*The door opens and Jessie, the model, comes in, wearing a dressing
gown. Maurice smiles at her, looking at her eagerly. As she's about to
remove her dressing gown she says:*

JESSIE

I can't do it with anyone I know watching.

Everyone looks at Maurice.

MAURICE

You've got to be professional now, my dear. I told you
earlier.

JESSIE

But I'm nervous.

MAURICE

So am I.

JESSIE

I am frightened! Okay!

39

TEACHER

Mr Russell . . . I think you might . . . If you don't mind . . .
could you please . . .

Everyone is looking at Maurice. He gets up.

MAURICE

Thank you and good night.

INT. SCHOOL CORRIDORS / ART ROOM. EVENING

*Maurice is roaming around the school. He goes to the door, and notices
a clear pane of glass, higher up. He stands on tiptoe to look through
the glass, holding on to the door handle at the same time. He sees
Jessie looking stiff and awkward, with a dressing gown around her, her
back exposed. Suddenly the door opens and he falls into the room with
a terrible clatter, knocking over various easels. Everyone turns and
looks at him.*

MAURICE

Everything all right?

EXT. TRAFALGAR SQUARE. DAY

They're walking together towards the National Gallery.

MAURICE

You won't be able to do it if you can't relax and let people
look at you. It's the human form, as it is, naked, in its
weakness and beauty.

JESSIE

Oh yeah.

MAURICE

What would your mother say?

JESSIE

She says if I weren't born she'd be better off.

MAURICE

Oh.

INT. NATIONAL GALLERY. DAY

They walk towards the Rokeby Venus.

MAURICE

There. You see?

JESSIE

My feet ache.

They stand in front of the picture.

Is Venus her name?

MAURICE

No. Venus is a goddess. Accompanied by Eros, she creates love and desire in us mortals, leading often to foolishness and despair. The usual shit. The thing about this Venus is, she was a real person, not a goddess. That's why people went crazy. (*Pause.*) For most men a woman's body is the most beautiful thing they will ever see.

JESSIE

Really? What is the most beautiful thing a girl sees? Eh? Do you know?

MAURICE

Her first child.

He looks at her. She is distressed.

Are you all right?

JESSIE

You don't think, do you!

He looks at her.

EXT. STEPS OF THE NATIONAL GALLERY. DAY

MAURICE

I'll take you out to lunch.

JESSIE

Take me somewhere posh.

MAURICE

Posh?

JESSIE

I want to meet someone really famous – not just you.

INT. SANDWICH BAR. DAY

Maurice and Jessie are sitting in a salt-beef sandwich bar, surrounded by signed photos of actors and comedians from the seventies and eighties.

JESSIE

Who are these bastards?

MAURICE

Some of these arseholes were very well known.

JESSIE

For what?

Maurice laughs.

MAURICE

You really cheer me up, you know.

JESSIE

You have a laugh at me, don't you?

MAURICE

Only a little.

JESSIE

I'll get you back.

MAURICE

You will.

JESSIE

Don't you worry. (*She eats enthusiastically.*) I'm not doing any more of that modelling, I can tell you that.

EXT. SOUTH BANK RIVERSIDE. DAY

> JESSIE

Do a bit then.

> MAURICE

Now?

> JESSIE

If you're so good at it.

Maurice clears his throat and prepares himself.

> MAURICE

'Is this a dagger which I see before me,
The handle toward my hand? Come, let me clutch thee –
I have thee not and yet I see thee still!'

Now tell me who wrote that?

> JESSIE

I don't know.

> MAURICE

Really?

> JESSIE

All right then, smart guy, what about this?

'I should be so lucky, lucky, lucky, lucky;
I should be so lucky . . .'

Well? Who wrote it?

> MAURICE

Not a clue.

> JESSIE

There you are then.

They laugh.

It's like a beach down there.

> MAURICE

I lived by the sea. As a child. It always calms me down.
Shall we go to the seaside, Venus?

43

                    JESSIE
    I'd rather go to Topshop.

INT. IAN'S FLAT. DAY

Ian lies on the sofa with his socks off and his trousers rolled up.
Maurice is cutting his toenails.

                    MAURICE
    Keep still, it's not an operation.

                    IAN
    I don't trust you.

                    MAURICE
    Got it! A palpable hit!

                    IAN
    But where has the little fucker gone!

                    MAURICE
    Who cares! It's free now!

                    IAN
    I can't have my home scattered with toenails. Look at the
    place! Since that minx has been staying here it has become
    a toilet.

                    MAURICE
    Oh God. I'll have to get my other glasses.

                    IAN
    They're round your neck.

INT. IAN'S FLAT LIVING ROOM. DAY

Maurice crawls around on the floor, with his glasses on, hunting for
the toenail.

                    IAN
    Over there!

                    MAURICE
    Where?

IAN

Under the table . . . that's it. No, further, further. (*Pause.*)
Maurice, I have to say, there's been a sliver – no more than
that, but a sliver – of relief.

MAURICE

There has?

IAN

You are a dear friend. I will leave you my books. Some of
them.

MAURICE

You'd better leave me your eyes too. Or just one of them.
(*Pause.*) Here it is – the elusive fucker!

He shows Ian the toenail before slipping it into his pocket.

IAN

How's Valerie?

MAURICE

Phoning me continuously with complaints.

IAN

You're her husband.

MAURICE

Am I?

IAN

You did one of your runners, if you remember.

MAURICE

Did I? But I've never wanted to be independent.

IAN

Oh, I love it.

MAURICE

I'm about to die and I know nothing about myself.

IAN

You have been loved, though, Maurice, you have been
adored.

45

MAURICE

Yes. And so have you, Ian, a little bit. Except you didn't always notice it.

Maurice gets to his feet and brushes himself down. He helps Ian, who is also getting up.

MAURICE

You can't cling to me like this, Ian, we'll both go down.

IAN

Put me on my feet then, you silly old fool!

MAURICE

You are on your feet.

IAN

Oh yes, thank you.

INT. IAN'S FLAT LIVING ROOM. DAY

The two old boys are arm-wrestling.

IAN

You're even weaker than me!

MAURICE

I am not!

IAN

There – I've won!

MAURICE

You did not. (*Pause.*) To keep the little minx away from you, I'm going to sacrifice my day by taking her shopping.

IAN

Marvellous.

MAURICE

But I need twenty quid for refreshments.

IAN

Done.

MAURICE

What will you do?

IAN

I need a lie down. She's exhausted me. I'm going to have a pre-nap nap.

MAURICE

Where is she?

IAN

Dead, I'm sure of it.

MAURICE

Are you absolutely certain?

IAN

There will be no sign of life for several hours. Shall we take some pills to celebrate?

MAURICE

Hold on. Let me check the coast is clear.

INT. IAN'S FLAT JESSIE'S ROOM. DAY

Maurice goes slowly into her bedroom. She is lying on her front, facing away from him, uncovered. Maurice puts his other glasses on and looks at her.

JESSIE

Don't do that.

MAURICE

You. (*Pause.*) Coming with me today?

JESSIE

You want me to?

She pulls the sheet over herself.

Okay.

MAURICE

Get up then.

                              JESSIE
I've got nothing to wear.

                              MAURICE
I can't think of anything more engaging, my dear.

EXT. SHOPS. DAY

Montage: Maurice and Jessie standing outside shops in Camden Town, Carnaby Street, Oxford Street. At each one she shakes her head at its appeal. He is getting more and more fagged out. The Christmas streets are crammed with shoppers.

EXT. SHOPPING STREET. DAY

The two of them stand outside another shop.

                              MAURICE
What's wrong with this shop?

                              JESSIE
It's all shit. I hate it.

                              MAURICE
Shall we have a couple of red ones to improve our mood?

                              JESSIE
No! (*Beat.*) I hate buying clothes.

                              MAURICE
But why?

                              JESSIE
How do I know!

                              MAURICE
Oh but Venus, you are lovely.

                              JESSIE
No I'm fucking not. I'll never be a model. It was all
rubbish. You did your best to help me. I wish you hadn't.
I let you down. I'll never be anything!

                               48

MAURICE

But you will look exquisite and absolutely luminous in a
new dress.

JESSIE

Does that mean see-through?

MAURICE

Bright – bright like a star!

She takes a deep breath.

JESSIE

Come on then.

INT. CHANGING ROOMS. DAY

*Maurice is standing outside the changing room. She throws out
rejected clothes which he attempts to gather up.*

JESSIE

If you try and look at me . . .

MAURICE

Look? I'm losing the will to live, Venus –

*Maurice doesn't know what to do with the clothes. He puts them on
the floor. She swishes the curtain open . . . and there she is, looking
rather transformed in a pretty dress.*

JESSIE

Does it suit me?

MAURICE

Yes, oh yes.

Jessie twirls around.

JESSIE

In what way?

MAURICE

In all possible ways. It goes with . . .

JESSIE

Yes?

MAURICE

Your nail varnish.

She's pleased.

INT. SHOP. DAY

They stand in the line to pay. Maurice dabs his sweating forehead.

JESSIE

What's the matter? We're nearly there.

INT. SHOP CHECKOUT. DAY

The Assistant is wrapping the dress in numerous bits of tissue paper. A huge carrier bag is presented.

ASSISTANT

How will you be paying, sir?

Jessie looks at Maurice. He fumbles for his wallet.

MAURICE

Oh I see . . . right . . . hold on.

At last he holds up his credit card. The Assistant inserts it into the machine. Maurice watches intently. The Assistant shakes her head.

ASSISTANT

It won't go through.

MAURICE

There must be some dirt stuck in your machine.

ASSISTANT

Did you say dirt? Do you have another card?

He scrambles through his pockets. At last he holds something up.

JESSIE

What's that?

MAURICE

One of your great uncle's toenail clippings.

JESSIE

Yuck!

MAURICE

Otherwise I'm afraid I've only got a twenty.

The Assistant takes the package and puts it on a shelf behind her.
Jessie bursts into tears.

Jessie!

She storms out of the shop. He follows.

EXT. OUTSIDE SHOP. DAY

JESSIE

You humiliated me!

She sticks her hand inside his jacket and pinches him hard.

MAURICE

Ow!

JESSIE

That'll teach you!

MAURICE

Jessie! Aren't we going to have lunch?

JESSIE

I never want to see you again!

MAURICE

Oh Venus, you're hurt and upset. I'll make it up to you.

JESSIE

Now I can never go back into that shop!

She pinches him again. His face twists in agony. He watches her go,
disappearing into the throng of Christmas shoppers.

INT. MAURICE'S FLAT LIVING ROOM. DAY

Maurice sits at his table with his shirt off, looking at his bruises. He
hears the letterbox rattle.

INT. MAURICE'S FLAT HALLWAY. DAY

Maurice goes to the front door, picks up a brown envelope, looks at it.

INT. MAURICE'S FLAT LIVING ROOM. DAY

Maurice sits at his table looking at the hospital letter.

INT. IAN'S FLAT. DAY

Maurice sits with Ian watching TV.

> MAURICE
>
> Where's the minger?

> IAN
>
> In her room.

> MAURICE
>
> Do you think she's going to come out?

> IAN
>
> She's been in there since yesterday. She didn't even come out for *Celebrity Love Island*. If it wasn't so relaxing I would be worried about her.

> MAURICE
>
> What do you think it is?

> IAN
>
> You're rather interested in all this, Maurice.

> MAURICE
>
> It's . . . it's just that I wanted her to pick up something for me.

> IAN
>
> No chance.

Maurice fingers the hospital envelope.

> What's that?

> MAURICE
>
> Nothing.

EXT. IAN'S FLAT. DAY

Maurice stands there looking up at Jessie's window. The curtains are closed. He picks up a stone and lobs it somewhat half-heartedly at the window. He turns and sees a kid on a bike staring at him.

INT. HOSPITAL. DAY

We follow a nurse along a ward. She is carrying various implements. She pulls the curtains on Maurice's bed.

NURSE

Ready?

She holds up the razor.

MAURICE

Christ! Will it hurt?

NURSE

Only if you struggle.

He throws back the covers and goes to pull his pyjama bottoms down.

The Nurse is shaving his pubic area.

INT. HOSPITAL. DAY

The doctor marks the spot where the incision will be.

INT. PRE-OP ROOM. DAY

Maurice is lying on the trolley outside the theatre.

SURGEON

Everything all right here? I've done hundreds of these. There's a strong chance of impotence and incontinence.

MAURICE

Oh.

SURGEON

You won't be dead. That is a result. (*To the Porters.*) Okay, let's get him to theatre.

As he is pushed along by two Porters.

> MAURICE
>
> I've always liked the theatre . . . very much liked the
> theatre . . . !

> PORTER
>
> Yeah, man.

INT. OPERATING THEATRE. DAY

*The Surgeons and their Assistants work on Maurice's old body. They
listen to pop music.*

INT. HOSPITAL. DAY

Ian sits beside Maurice's hospital bed.

> IAN
>
> Why didn't you tell me?

> MAURICE
>
> Oh, you know. I didn't want to think about it. I hate
> sympathy.

> IAN
>
> But you wouldn't have got any from me.

> MAURICE
>
> I know. You're a true friend. How's the nurse?

> IAN
>
> She's not nurse material. Anyway, I told her to be on her
> way.

> MAURICE
>
> You did?

> IAN
>
> It's agony for both of us.

> MAURICE
>
> When is she off?

                                IAN

As soon as possible.

                              MAURICE

Where will she go?

                                IAN

That's up to her. They always need people in Africa I hear.

Ian picks up Maurice's glasses.

It hardly seems worth going home.

                              MAURICE

What are you doing?

                                IAN

Polishing your glasses. (*Pause.*) So you can see to read.

                              MAURICE

Oh Ian . . .

                                IAN

When are you coming out?

                              MAURICE

Sooner than you think.

INT. HOSPITAL. DAY

Later. Maurice is pulling his clothes out of the bedside cupboard.

INT. HOSPITAL. DAY

*Having dressed and put the rest of his things in a plastic bag, Maurice
now stands at the Nurses' desk. Maurice bangs on the counter where
the Nurses are stationed.*

                              MAURICE

Why not! I am a free man!

                               NURSE

We wouldn't advise it so soon after an operation. Why don't
you wait to see the doctor?

                                 55

MAURICE

Because there are people I need to see!

NURSE

Can't they come here?

MAURICE

No!

EXT. IAN'S FLAT. DAY

Maurice stands outside with his bag. He rings the doorbell. Jessie opens it.

JESSIE

Hello!

MAURICE

Hello, Jessie.

JESSIE

It's you.

She smiles.

MAURICE

Yes, it is more or less – *moi*.

INT. IAN'S FLAT HALLWAY. DAY

Maurice holds out his arm while she cuts off the hospital wristband.

MAURICE

I was afraid you'd gone.

JESSIE

He hasn't managed to get rid of me yet. Why didn't you tell me you were having an operation?

MAURICE

I didn't want to cheer you up.

She cuts the band off.

Free at last!

INT. IAN'S FLAT LIVING ROOM. DAY

Maurice is now sitting with Ian, watching football.

MAURICE
I'm battered. D'you think she'd cut my toenails?

IAN
I wouldn't let her near my body with anything sharp.

MAURICE
No.

IAN
What's that smell?

MAURICE
A little cologne from Paris.

IAN
Get rid of it! It's making me vertiginous!

Jessie comes out with a tray on which there are beers, crisps, nuts, and a cup of tea for Ian.

JESSIE
Drinks, gentlemen?

IAN
This is unusual, Jessie. Are you on Ketamine, GBH or just the mushrooms?

Jessie laughs at this.

(*To Maurice.*) You see, Maurice, I am contemporary.

MAURICE
At last.

She walks in front of the TV. A goal is scored. Ian waves at her to get out of the way.

IAN
I can't see!

JESSIE
What?

IAN

Put it down! Not there!

JESSIE

Where?

IAN

There! Oh God, I can't breathe!

JESSIE

Stop shouting then.

IAN

I can't get through to you otherwise!

Ian takes the tea and looks at it.

Ahhhh!

JESSIE

What now?

MAURICE

Ian – are you all right?

IAN

Everyone knows you don't put milk in lemon tea!

JESSIE

You like milk.

IAN

I've told you, only on my cereal. Not in anything else.

JESSIE

You have milk in your hot chocolate.

IAN

Yes, but – Oh, I'm exhausted. Fan me, Maurice, before
I expire.

Jessie offers a bowl.

JESSIE

Nuts anyone?

*She looks at them wickedly. Then she snatches a beer and goes into the
kitchen.*

                              IAN
        I can't wait to get back to work. I'll take anything.

                            MAURICE
        Really?

                              IAN
        Except corpses – I don't need that.

                            MAURICE
        I think I've pretty much cornered the market there.

                              IAN
        If I don't get anything I'll write my memoirs.

                            MAURICE
        That shouldn't take you long.

                              IAN
        What? (*Pause.*) What do you do to her – at your age?

                            MAURICE
        It's a very difficult thing – but I'm nice to her.

                              IAN
        You've always had charm, Maurice.

                            MAURICE
        Have I?

                              IAN
        I've always envied it.

Pause.

                            MAURICE
        I'll make you some tea.

Maurice goes into the kitchen.

INT. IAN'S FLAT KITCHEN. DAY

Jessie is sitting there smoking. Maurice puts the kettle on, watching her.

                            MAURICE
        I will die soon. Venus, can I touch your hand?

JESSIE

That's one chat-up line I haven't heard.

MAURICE

I'm impotent, of course.

JESSIE

Thank Christ.

MAURICE

But I can still take a theoretical interest.

JESSIE

Have you been thinking about me?

MAURICE

All the time I was in hospital.

JESSIE

What did you think about me?

MAURICE

I saw your body.

JESSIE

Which part?

MAURICE

Your hair. Your feet. Your legs. Your behind. Your eyes.

JESSIE

My eyes.

MAURICE

Your elbows. Your cunt.

JESSIE

My cunt.

MAURICE

Yes. Whether it's one of those – one of those particularly
lovely and . . .

JESSIE

Shut up. (*Pause.*) You can touch my hand.

He takes her hand and goes to kiss it.

> Only with your fingers! Anything else will make me
> vomitous.

*He holds and strokes her hands and fingers, as well as her wrist and
the hairs on her arms.*

MAURICE

Can I ask you, have you ever been loved before?

She looks at him.

JESSIE

Yes. Yes. Not long ago. If you can call it love.

He looks at her. She looks away, thinking.

INT. MAURICE'S FLAT. DAY

He is on the phone to his agent.

MAURICE

I can do it. I want to do it. I am well enough. I need the
money too. (*Pause.*) Thanks, thanks. (*Pause.*) But I will
need a big car. An enormous fucker.

INT. CAR. DAY

Maurice and Jessie sit in a big chauffeur-driven car, going to the set.

JESSIE

You must be really famous.

MAURICE

Oh I am, I am.

The Chauffeur looks at them in his mirror.

Maurice leafs through the script but can't find his bit.

> It's a pretty important role. The lynchpin of the story. It's a
> speaking part, too. (*To Jessie.*) I'll explain everything to you,
> as we go. I think you should work in films.

JESSIE

Do you?

MAURICE

Definitely.

JESSIE
(*to the Driver*)
Can we open the roof?

The Driver opens a panel in the roof and she stands up and sticks her head through it.

EXT. STREET. DAY

We see the car coming down the street with the girl's head sticking out of the top.

INT. CAR. DAY

Inside. Maurice sits there looking up her skirt.

MAURICE
(*to the Driver*)
Turn it up, my man! More vol–ume!!

He sings along happily to the music.

INT. TRAILER. DAY

Maurice and Jessie sit in a big trailer holding scripts. She is going through his lines with him.

JESSIE
'Where are we going, my love?'

MAURICE
'To the wildest and loneliest place in the world. To discover finally which it is, men or women, who are the most unfaithful.'

JESSIE
You remembered all that.

MAURICE

It happens to be my job, remembering other people's
words.

JESSIE

But how did you remember all that?

There is a knock on the door of the trailer and a Runner comes in.

RUNNER

We're ready when you are, Mr Russell.

INT. FILM SET. DAY

*A sitting room. Paris – mid-eighteenth century. An Old Man (Maurice)
with a young male Assistant.*

OLD MAN

You will see how fickle men are in love, just like women.

ASSISTANT

I will not believe it until I see it with my own eyes.

OLD MAN

They come.

A young couple run on, arguing.

WOMAN

You are in love with another?

MAN

I don't love you!

WOMAN

But my body cannot do without your hands!

She tears at her clothes. The Old Man comes out with his Assistant.

OLD MAN

You see, as I said, that when it comes to love –

He falters, confused.

DIRECTOR

Cut. What's up? Bring a chair.

MAURICE

It is hot. These clothes are heavy.

He gets up unsteadily.

INT. STUDIO. DAY

Maurice and Jessie sit together on the edge of the set watching the Actress. She is alone now, reading a letter.

Jessie pours more water for Maurice as they watch the scene.

ACTRESS

'I'm sorry, my love, but we must part for good, I am not the man to make you happy, and so I must say goodbye . . .'

Maurice watches Jessie watching the actress. She is amazed.

INT. TRAILOR. DAY

Maurice is getting changed. Jessie is with him.

JESSIE

How did she do it? I could never have done that.

MAURICE

I'm sure you could. Mind you, she's terribly pretty.

JESSIE

Am I not?

MAURICE

Oh Venus –

JESSIE

Now you've upset me. Jesus, Maurice, don't you ever learn?

MAURICE

Sorry.

JESSIE

You will be.

MAURICE

My dear, will you pass me my trousers.

JESSIE

What's that?

MAURICE

A catheter.

JESSIE

Oh God, yuck.

MAURICE

I think it's leaking.

JESSIE

I don't want it on my shoes! You're always dripping,
Maurice!

MAURICE

Hold on –

JESSIE

I'm not touching that! There's always bits of you where
there shouldn't be!

A knock on the door.

Put it away!

MAURICE

Pass me that towel!

She does so.

JESSIE

I wonder what I'll be like when I'm old.

MAURICE

I wish I could be there to see.

An Assistant comes in and gives him an envelope.

ASSISTANT

You asked for cash.

MAURICE

Thank you, my dear. (*He pats his pocket.*) I wonder if the
shops are still open.

EXT. STREET. NIGHT

They stand outside a jeweller's shop with a glittering Christmas display.

                    JESSIE
You think they'll suit me?

                    MAURICE
I don't know. Let me look at your ears.

He looks.

Perfect – like seashells, Venus.

                    JESSIE
Really? (*Pause.*) But don't touch.

                    MAURICE
I know, I know.

                    JESSIE
Let's go in then. You got the bloody money this time?

INT. MAURICE'S FLAT. EVENING

Jessie stands in front of a mirror trying on new earrings.

                    JESSIE
I'm going to wear these tonight.

                    MAURICE
Venus, you will look like a movie star.

                    JESSIE
Sometimes you make me feel warm inside.

                    MAURICE
I do?

He kisses her neck.

Is there an old-man odour?

                    JESSIE
Not so much this evening.

MAURICE

I wonder why.

JESSIE

You can kiss my shoulders.

MAURICE

Can I?

JESSIE

Three kisses. Three, I said! No licking or burping, you dirty filthy old shithead.

MAURICE

Oh you please me.

JESSIE

And you me!

He puts his hands on her breasts. She elbows him in the stomach. He staggers about, holding his guts.

MAURICE

Steady on, I'm just out of intensive care.

JESSIE

You ask for it, Maurice, you know you do, with your forwardness. (*Pause.*) Maurice. Don't you believe in anything?

MAURICE

You'd think I'd have something to pass on during this last five minutes of my life. Pleasure, I like. I've tried to give pleasure. That's all I'd recommend to anyone.

She is looking at him intently.

JESSIE

You've made me sticky with your slug tongue. I think I'll have a bath, before I put my new clothes on.

MAURICE

A bath here?

67

                              JESSIE
    Yes.

                             MAURICE
    Well, well. I'll run it for you.

                              JESSIE
    Would you?

                             MAURICE
    With pleasure.

INT. MAURICE'S BATHROOM. EVENING

Maurice rushes around, finding bath salts, smellies, a shower cap,
looking around as she goes into his bedroom, and closes the door
behind her.

INT. MAURICE'S BATHROOM. EVENING

He is cleaning the bath, clearly something he's never done before.

INT. MAURICE'S BATHROOM. EVENING

The bath is full. He tests it with his elbow. He is on his knees,
crouching by the bath, when she comes in, wearing one of Maurice's
dressing gowns.

                              JESSIE
    Out you go. Wouldn't want to over-stimulate your heart.

                             MAURICE
    No, no.

                              JESSIE
    If you try and look I'll rip your eyes out and stick them up
    your arse.

                             MAURICE
    I wouldn't hope for anything less.

INT. MAURICE'S FLAT HALLWAY. EVENING

She is in the bath. Maurice approaches the bathroom door with a chair. He sits down outside the bathroom door.

MAURICE

You say this local man – he was a farmer, older than you, right? – he was not kind?

JESSIE

He was kind to me. For a time. He promised me things. He bought me stuff. He took me on a train. We went to a hotel. We had champagne. There were roses.

MAURICE

Then you got pregnant.

JESSIE

Does everyone know?

MAURICE

I'm not a complete fool. It's happened to girls before.

JESSIE

Then . . . then he stopped being kind. He went the other way. A long way that way.

MAURICE

He was nasty?

JESSIE

Why would anyone be like that? It wasn't a miscarriage. Mum called it that. It was an abortion. She made me.

She weeps.

MAURICE

Terrible. Terrible to lose a child in any way.

JESSIE

Yes, yes.

He sits there listening to her snivel.

MAURICE

Oh you darling girl, Venus. You darling.

INT. MAURICE'S FLAT BATHROOM. EVENING

As she gets out of the bath and reaches for a towel and dries her face, she hears, through the door, his voice:

> MAURICE
'Shall I compare thee to a summer's day?
Thou art more lovely and more temperate:
Rough winds do shake the darling buds of May' *etc.*

INT. MAURICE'S FLAT HALLWAY. EVENING

She comes out of the bathroom wrapped in a towel, with her hair down. He lays a towel on the floor for her to step onto. Then he hands her a glass of champagne.

> JESSIE
Thank you.

> MAURICE
You look wonderful. Radiant, startling . . . ravishing.

> JESSIE
Oh do I?

INT. MAURICE'S FLAT. EVENING

Later. Jessie is finishing getting dressed, doing up her shoes. Maurice watches her, sitting there with her other shoe on his lap.

> JESSIE
The story I just told you.

> MAURICE
Yes.

> JESSIE
You don't think I'm low, do you?

> MAURICE
No. You doubt yourself, Jessie, don't you? Here.

He holds out her shoe.

Let's walk a little and then we'll have dinner. I know such a good place along the river. Lots of celebrities go there.

                              JESSIE

Who?

                              MAURICE
                             (*thinks*)

Ant and Dec.

                              JESSIE

Really.

                              MAURICE

We can pick up a cab on the street.

                              JESSIE

No, Maurice. I'm going out.

                              MAURICE

Oh what a shame. Anywhere nice?

                              JESSIE

A party.

                              MAURICE

Alone?

                              JESSIE

With some friends.

                              MAURICE

Jolly good. Which friends?

                              JESSIE

Keep your nose out.

                              MAURICE

Of course. You can go to the party for an hour and we can meet later.

                              JESSIE

It's an all-night party.

                              MAURICE

Right. How will you stay up all night?

                              JESSIE
    I'll manage.

                             MAURICE
    But Ian will worry.

                              JESSIE
    It's all right. I've asked him already. He was pleased to get
    rid of me. I don't think he likes me very much.

                             MAURICE
    Doesn't he? But I like you, Venus. I like you. I love you.

                              JESSIE
    Bye.

                             MAURICE
    Can we do something tomorrow?

                              JESSIE
    Maybe. If you want.

At the door.

    Thanks for the earrings.

INT. MAURICE'S FLAT. NIGHT

Maurice sits in his flat, staring at the paintings on the wall.

INT. MAURICE'S FLAT. DAY

Maurice is eating his breakfast. He looks at the wall again.

EXT. STREET. DAY

*We see Maurice walking along the street with a parcel wrapped in
newspaper.*

EXT. OUTSIDE GALLERY. DAY

Maurice approaches the gallery and goes in.

INT. GALLERY. DAY

He walks across the vast sterile space. A Girl gets up from the desk and goes to him.

INT. BACK ROOM IN THE GALLERY. DAY

Maurice sits opposite his Art Collector friend, showing him the painting.

> MAURICE
> You've always liked it.

> ART COLLECTOR
> I might sell it on, but I'd like to buy it for myself.

> MAURICE
> Would it be cash?

> ART COLLECTOR
> If you want. What's up?

> MAURICE
> Family problems, you know. The peck, peck, peck of vultures.

> ART COLLECTOR
> What sort of vultures?

> MAURICE
> Big fuckers.

> ART COLLECTOR
> With red nail varnish?

> MAURICE
> Vultures come in all shapes and sizes.

> ART COLLECTOR
> Yes, I've noticed.

EXT. STREET. EVENING

Maurice strolls along the street, which is full of Christmas decorations. People are stumbling around with Christmas trees, as they do. Maurice is rather cheerful.

EXT. STREET. EVENING

He turns a corner and runs into Valerie, who is making her way slowly, on two sticks, carrying a plastic bag.

MAURICE

Valerie – what are you doing?

VALERIE

Trying to get home, Maurice.

MAURICE

Let me . . .

He takes her shopping bag and looks inside it.

Sausage rolls and yogurt.

VALERIE

I can't carry any more.

MAURICE

I shall come and cook for you.

VALERIE

Stop making a fuss.

MAURICE

Let me help you then.

She takes the bag and he tries to take it back from her.

VALERIE

No, I'm all right, Maurice.

MAURICE

At least take a taxi.

VALERIE

I can't afford taxis. I've just had a quote for that damn boiler.

MAURICE

I should . . .

VALERIE

I can't stop. I've presents to wrap.

She starts off down the street again. He watches her and pats his pockets. She calls back to him:

Are you going to Michael's tomorrow?

MAURICE

Probably.

INT. MICHAEL'S HOUSE. DAY

Maurice is at Christmas lunch with his grown-up son, wife, kids and friends. A long noisy table. Maurice is sitting there rather isolated as everyone talks, laughs, disputes. At last his son addresses him.

MICHAEL

Dad, Dad – this'll make you laugh. Marcia's father, he's a game old goer, as we know – puts his hand on John's assistant's knee. She must be at least thirty-five years younger than him. And he says, 'My dear, where do we go from here?' She removes his hand, rather politely, and says, 'I'm going home, but I could call you an ambulance!'

They all laugh. Maurice sits there.

Thank God you were never like that.

INT. MICHAEL'S HOUSE STUDY. DAY

A small room, enclosed by books. Rather furtively, Maurice is whispering into the phone.

MAURICE

Meet me, please meet me, four o'clock by the Round Pond, on the Heath. You'll find it.

EXT. MICHAEL'S HOUSE. DAY

Maurice is hurrying down the front path, his family at the door and windows, waving to him.

CHILD

See you next year, Grandad!

EXT. THE HEATH. AFTERNOON

He sits there. The light is fading.

INT./EXT. PHONE BOX. AFTERNOON

Maurice speaks to Ian.

> MAURICE
> Happy Christmas, dear Ian. Yes, I might come by later. Has
> Donald got me another hot water bottle? (*Pause.*) You . . .
> er . . . cooking for the minger? Is she there?

> IAN
> Thank Christ, no. She just went out, in her finest Argos
> bling, with some sullen boy.

> MAURICE
> Right.

INT. MAURICE'S FLAT. DAY

*He sits at his living-room table, feeling awful. He looks up and sees
Jessie at the window. She knocks but he ignores her. She knocks again
and he lets her in.*

> MAURICE
> I'm absurd – a repulsive fool. Why would you be interested
> in me?

> JESSIE
> What?

INT. MAURICE'S FLAT. DAY

They sit across the table from one another.

> JESSIE
> You can smell my neck.

> MAURICE
> Can I?

JESSIE

You can. No kissing. That would make me never come
back.

MAURICE

I understand.

She goes over to him and holds up her hair, as he kisses her neck.

JESSIE

You like to do this, don't you?

MAURICE

Yes. There really isn't anything else.

JESSIE

I know what you want me for, but you'll never ever get it.
I like you trying. But I do want to give you a little treat.
A Christmas present.

MAURICE

That was yesterday.

JESSIE

I want to cheer you up.

MAURICE

Yes, but how? How?

JESSIE

Watch.

*She puts her hand between her legs, pressing her finger into her cunt.
She holds her finger up, inviting him to smell it.*

MAURICE

What have you come here for?

JESSIE

To see you.

MAURICE

You want more money?

JESSIE

I like it when you give me things.

MAURICE

I've noticed. (*Pause.*) Happy Christmas.

INT. TATTOO PARLOUR. DAY

Maurice sits there watching as Jessie has a tattoo done on her lower back.

MAURICE

A dove would have been out of place in that position.
The serpent represents energy itself. Of course, it has a
threatening tongue, a vicious hiss and a tendency to
suffocate its victims – but it also represents the wisdom
of the deep . . .

She looks at him. Then he notices she is looking past him at a Boy on the street.

EXT. STREET. DAY

He follows her but she walks ahead of him.

MAURICE

Jessie!

He sees now that the Boy has joined her.

Jessie! Jessie!

He holds on to a fence to steady himself, out of breath and almost exhausted. Jessie comes to him.

Go with him . . . go. You should. Here . . .

He gives her money.

JESSIE

Thank you. Thank you.

She hurries off. He stands there, watching her put her arms around the Boy and kiss him.

INT. PUB. DAY

Maurice stands at the bar.

> MAURICE
> *(to the Barman)*
> The red one, please.

INT. PUB. DAY

Maurice sits there gloomily drinking a Bacardi Breezer. Ian knocks on the window and comes in.

> IAN
> You look rather forlorn.

> MAURICE
> What?

> IAN
> Come on.

EXT. STREET. DAY

The two old men bowl along in the back of a black cab.

> IAN
> I've been missing you.

> MAURICE
> You have?

INT. THE GARRICK CLUB. DAY

The two of them going slowly up the stairs.

> MAURICE
> This is a rare treat, my friend.

> IAN
> There are no pockets in a shroud.

INT. THE GARRICK CLUB. DAY

The two of them sitting in huge chairs by the fireplace with large glasses of whisky.

> MAURICE

Cheers, old boy.

> IAN

Yes, yes.

> MAURICE

Fond of you.

> IAN

Me too.

> MAURICE

We shall not see our like again.

> IAN

Nor shall we. In a world of Kylie, Snoop Dog, and Atomic Vagina, who remembers Johnny G?

> MAURICE

Not me.

> IAN

Nor me.

They drink.

> MAURICE

It was '62 when I first saw you.

> IAN

It was?

> MAURICE

You were a strapping Laertes.

> IAN

Strapping? Yes, sounds like me.

> MAURICE

The Ophelia was something of a minger. She wore a kilt, if I'm not mistaken.

IAN

Bloody Peter Hall . . .

They drink some more.

I love this horrible place. Reminds me of what I wanted to become.

MAURICE

You've had a good innings.

IAN

I never found love, or it didn't find me. I never became the actor I wanted to be. I think I lived the wrong life entirely. You should have warned me, years ago. (*Pause.*) Maurice, you're not by any chance, you know, interested in Jessie? Eh?

Maurice laughs.

MAURICE

I absolutely hate the sight of her – indeed of anybody young, as you know very well. If I've taken a slight interest it was only because you begged me to entertain the little minx. All that shopping, it was for you, Ian.

IAN

Thought so. (*Pause.*) Haven't seen enough of you lately, old boy. I like your ring, your hands . . .

MAURICE

Another large one?

EXT. STREET. DAY

They are walking down the street together, quite drunk.

MAURICE

Come on – I've got a great idea.

IAN

What?

INT. ST PAUL'S CHURCH. DAY

They are in the Actor's Church. They walk along the line of plaques.

                    IAN
They're running out of room here.

                    MAURICE
Luckily Ian isn't a long name.

A quartet is rehearsing. They suddenly decide to do a run-through. As they begin, Maurice takes holds of Ian.

Shall we?

                    IAN
Oh yes.

They dance together happily, a little waltz. Then Maurice becomes flustered and looks at his watch.

Time for your injection?

                    MAURICE
I have to be somewhere.

EXT. SUPERMARKET. DAY

Maurice staggers out of a supermarket with several bags full of shopping.

INT. VALERIE'S HOUSE KITCHEN. DAY

He starts to unpack food and champagne.

                    VALERIE
I've forgotten – did I invite you?

                    MAURICE
No, I invited you. And I wanted to see you.

                    VALERIE
You did? Good God.

INT. VALERIE'S HOUSE KITCHEN. DAY

He opens the champagne. Meanwhile things are cooking. She calls him from the other room.

> VALERIE
>
> Maurice, Maurice, quickly!

He goes to her.

> MAURICE
>
> Why do you keep shouting when I am cooking?

> VALERIE
>
> Look, there's you! On TV!

> MAURICE
>
> Oh Christ.

> VALERIE
>
> How handsome you were! And there's that woman.

> MAURICE
>
> Yes, yes.

> VALERIE
>
> Who took you away from us.

> MAURICE
>
> It's burning –

He dashes back.

> VALERIE
> (*shouts out*)
>
> You will burn, Maurice.

> MAURICE
> (*off*)
>
> Yes, dear.

INT. VALERIE'S HOUSE LIVING ROOM. DAY

She eats. He sits there watching her. He pours her more champagne.

MAURICE

You were a good mother. I rather left you holding the babies, didn't I?

VALERIE

You did do that. Three children under six, to be exact.

MAURICE

I can see it must have been . . . inconvenient.

VALERIE

That you put your own pleasure first.

MAURICE

Will you forgive me?

VALERIE

Forgotten rather than forgiven.

MAURICE

I did love you. For a time. And for the rest of the time, I was fond of you. More than fond of you.

VALERIE

Please don't say all this, you don't have to, I don't want it –

MAURICE

It's my goodbye to you.

VALERIE

Why, where are you going?

MAURICE

We won't live for ever –

VALERIE

No.

He falls to his knees beside her and bows his head. She caresses his hair. He touches her – her face, neck, hair – and then he kisses her, properly, on the mouth. They stare at one another.

INT. MAURICE'S FLAT. NIGHT

Maurice finds himself in the same position as at the beginning of the film, sitting on the end of his bed, alone.

INT. CAFÉ. DAY

Maurice is sitting in their usual café. He looks up to see Ian and Donald come in. He becomes bewildered and then angry as Ian sits at another table and insists Donald sit with him. Ian pointedly turns his back to Maurice. Maurice makes up his mind and then gets up and goes over to them.

                    MAURICE
You insult me.

                    IAN
On the contrary, the insult is on the other side.

                    MAURICE
How so?

                    IAN
Do I look like a fool? Do I! Answer me!

                    MAURICE
Don't tempt me today. I haven't had my tranquilliser yet.

                    IAN
You are easily tempted, as we know. I have been
questioning my niece's daughter very closely – in search of
the facts.

                    MAURICE
So what? What could I have done? You begged me to find
her work –

                    IAN
But you have degraded the girl!

                    MAURICE
Surely the sitters for Gauguin and Matisse wouldn't be
considered – er . . .

                    DONALD
Mingers . . .

                    MAURICE
What? Yes –

85

IAN

You say minger to me! Jessie is a shy provincial girl – to take advantage of such a vulnerable young person, to take her to drinking establishments, ply her with alcohol –

MAURICE

It's she who plies me –

IAN

I doubt that very much. And then to . . .

MAURICE

To what?

IAN

I hate to imagine how far you might have gone with someone so fragile, so easily led on –

Maurice indicates his nuts.

MAURICE

There's nothing you can do with nothing! Have a peep!

He starts to undo his trousers.

IAN

Oh put it away – no one wants to see nothing, you wretched man!

MAURICE

I'll slap you with what's there!

IAN

I don't think so, dear!

DONALD

Maurice – please – we come here every day – they bring us croissants with our coffee!

MAURICE
(*to Ian*)

You didn't welcome her! You called her vile!

IAN

That is a lie!

86

DONALD

Ian, old man, you have to admit you did have one or two
little reservations about her character –

IAN

How dare you! What the hell do you mean – reservations?

DONALD

You handed her that halibut and expected her to –

IAN

To what? To cook it. That's all. That's perverted exploitation?
(*He points at Maurice.*) But to be so desperate, to behave
without respect for me or my family –

Maurice taps Ian on the top of the head with his newspaper.

Now you strike me! (*To Donald.*) Did you see? I have been
struck!

MAURICE

Get some sense into your thick skull before you die, Ian!

IAN

You venomous rat!

DONALD

Guys – guys – think! Where are we going with this?

IAN

A dying man!

MAURICE

A fool too!

IAN

Let's have you –

MAURICE

Come on!

IAN

I'll take you on!

MAURICE

To the death then!

The two of them struggle. Donald intervenes, as does their usual Waitress.

> DONALD
> Boys, boys. Come on now, what is this, catheters at dawn?

> IAN
> Oh shut up!

> WAITRESS
> I'm going to have to bar you two troublemakers.

> IAN
> He started it –

> MAURICE
> I did not!

> IAN
> You hit me!

> WAITRESS
> Out!

> MAURICE
> It's okay – I'm going.

EXT. PARK. DAY

Maurice sits on a bench watching kids with their new electrical toys as fathers study instruction leaflets. He is very upset.

INT. MAURICE'S FLAT. DAY

Maurice opens the door.

> MAURICE
> You've come back!

> JESSIE
> I've brought a friend.

Maurice looks out to see a Young Man sitting on a wall opposite.

> Can we come in?

INT. MAURICE'S FLAT. DAY

Jessie is sitting there. Maurice sits there. The Young Man walks about, looking at things, picking them up.

> YOUNG MAN
>
> Have you really met Ricky Gervais?

INT. MAURICE'S FLAT. DAY

The Young Man sits on the sofa with his legs apart, looking at Maurice.

> YOUNG MAN
>
> Go on, ask him.

> JESSIE
>
> Maurice, would you like to go for a little walk?

> MAURICE
>
> With you, Venus?

> JESSIE
>
> No. On your own.

> MAURICE
>
> Exercise is good for some people, I've heard.

> YOUNG MAN
>
> Yeah.

> MAURICE
>
> What will you do?

EXT. SHOPPING STREET. DAY

Street is crowded with shoppers going to the sales: gaudy Christmas decorations.

EXT. REGENT'S PARK. DAY

He's walking along the canal path.

EXT. REGENT'S PARK. DAY

He finds a broken gate; he enters the Open Air Theatre, which is deserted.

EXT. REGENT'S PARK OPEN AIR THEATRE. DAY

Maurice comes into the deserted auditorium. A fox is sitting on the stage. They eye each other cautiously . . . and the fox saunters off slowly into the bushes. Maurice sits in the auditorium in different seats. He thinks. He goes up onto the stage and faces the empty seats.

MAURICE
'To be or not to be, that is the question . . .'

Maurice is very still as he considers this question.

EXT. STREET. DAY

Maurice hurries back to his flat.

INT. MAURICE'S FLAT. DAY

He comes into the house. The place is wrecked; there are bottles, crisp packets, chairs knocked over. He goes towards the bedroom.

INT. MAURICE'S BEDROOM. DAY

He appears at the door. From under a sheet they look at him raving.

MAURICE
No, no! Out! Out!

INT. MAURICE'S SITTING ROOM. DAY

Later.

YOUNG MAN
You invited us in, old man.

JESSIE
That's right.

The Young Man is looking through Maurice's wallet. He takes the little money that is there. On the table is a Toby jug, in which Maurice keeps his money. Jessie glances at it – Maurice sees her – but says nothing.

Come on, let's go.

> YOUNG MAN
> And you are a dirty, dirty old man.

> MAURICE
> And you are on your way. Get out!

He picks up a walking stick and charges at the Young Man, hitting him on the head with the stick.

The Young Man examines his head.

> YOUNG MAN
> I'm bleedin' bleeding now!

As Maurice goes to attack the boy again, Jessie pushes Maurice down. He collapses onto the floor.

> JESSIE
> *(to the Boy)*
> You stupid bastard – what have you done?

As he lies there the Young Man takes some things. She pulls him away and the two of them leave.

EXT. STREET OUTSIDE MAURICE'S FLAT. DAY

Jessie and the Young Man come out of the house. She pulls him by the arm and they hurry away.

INT. MAURICE'S FLAT. NIGHT

Maurice lies there semi-conscious. Then we see a hand move and he tries to put his weight on his arms.

INT. CLUB. NIGHT

We see Jessie and the Young Man pushing their way into a crowded noisy club.

INT. MAURICE'S FLAT. NIGHT

Maurice sees the phone, which is on a little table in the distance. It feels miles away. He crawls for a while. Then, exhausted, he lies on his back, staring at a picture of him in some play, years ago.

INT. CLUB. NIGHT

The Boy, facing the wall, pushes E pills into his face. He turns to Jessie and encourages her to take some. She is upset, and refuses.

INT. MAURICE'S FLAT. NIGHT

Maurice has moved a little, closer to the phone, bringing himself into line with another picture. The Bristol Old Vic – a poster from the sixties.

INT. CLUB. NIGHT

The Young Man attempts to pull Jessie out onto the dance floor, but she doesn't want to dance. They argue but we can't hear what they're saying.

INT. MAURICE'S FLAT. NIGHT

Maurice lies there absolutely still – looking at a photograph of Valerie as a young woman.

INT. CLUB. NIGHT

The Young Man is dancing. His face is blazing. She is not there.

INT. MAURICE'S FLAT. NIGHT

Maurice has made it to the Shakespeare Toby jug. The bearded face seems to mock him.

EXT. STREET OUTSIDE CLUB. NIGHT

We see her running out of the club.

INT. MAURICE'S FLAT. NIGHT

He is now tantalisingly close to the phone. With his last ounce of energy he stretches for it . . . and misses. He rolls onto his back and sees a painting on the wall of a family on a pebbly beach. A little boy is throwing a pebble.

EXT. WEST END STREET. NIGHT

Jessie tries to hail a cab. She is a mess, behaving wildly in the middle of the street.

INT. MAURICE'S FLAT. DAWN

There is a tremendous banging on the door. Then the same on the windows. Maurice lies there, not responding, eyes closed.

EXT. MAURICE'S FLAT. DAWN

Jessie sits on the pavement and cries.

INT. IAN'S FLAT. DAY

Jessie sits at the table, smoking, trembling, wearing the same clothes, tear-stained. Ian is with her, furious.

> IAN
> Tell me the truth now! I have to know everything!

> JESSIE
> Why?

> IAN
> Something's been going on behind my back.

> JESSIE
> Like the whole world, Ian –

> IAN
> Less of that, miss. Has he been touching you?

She shakes her head.

> But you just said he touched your hand . . .

JESSIE

A little . . .

IAN

How can he touch you a little! Is this how he rewarded you?

He puts his hand in his pocket and takes out the earrings, which he shows to her.

JESSIE

Where did you find those?

IAN

In your socks where you put them.

JESSIE

Why were you –

IAN

I am fucking *in loco parentis* here! They're yours, then?

JESSIE

He bought them for me –

IAN

He's a pensioner! He's an actor! Do you know how much these cost? Why would he buy something like this for you unless you wanted him to?

She sits there petrified.

JESSIE

We went to a few places.

IAN

Is that right? Was it only that? I've been let down, and I've got high blood pressure, Jessie, I could die like that. (*He snaps his fingers.*) At any moment!

JESSIE

So could he, but he gets about.

IAN

Clearly. What did that gullible old fool want from you?

JESSIE

Stop going on about him like this!

IAN

What?

JESSIE

He's dead! He's fucking dead!

The phone rings in another room. Ian just stares at her. As he gets up to answer it we close in on Jessie.

INT. MAURICE'S LIVING ROOM. DAY

Jessie sits there bolt upright, scared. Ian stands there incredulous, fuming. From the bedroom we hear the noise of Paramedics attending to Maurice, the sound of Police communicating over radios. There are voices from the bedroom, which contains Maurice, Policemen, Paramedics and the GP.

IAN

Are you responsible for this?

He stares at her. The Policeman comes out.

POLICEMAN

Can I have a word?

Jessie stands up.

Apparently there was an intruder, though there's no sign of forced entry. He was knocked down.

IAN

Who was it?

POLICEMAN

I asked him for a description and all he said was, 'He was damned ugly.'

Ian stares at Jessie, but she says nothing. The Paramedics have come back into the room and start to pack up their gear, talking amongst themselves. The Policeman begins a noisy conversation on his walkie-talkie.

White male in his early seventies . . . Russell, Maurice . . . (*He spells the name letter by letter.*) No sign of forced entry . . .

The Doctor comes in, talking on his mobile phone.

95

DOCTOR

He's badly bruised and he's shaken up. There's nothing broken. He needs to rest. I have to take him in . . . If the worst comes to the worst, tomorrow morning will be okay but he can't stay here alone. Hang on a minute . . .

The Doctor addresses Ian.

I'm having some trouble getting a bed . . . he needs someone with him. Are you . . . ?

IAN

No, of course not. I could die at any moment myself, I've got high blood pressure, I've got chronic anxiety, burning indigestion and . . . and –

DOCTOR

Okay, right –

From the next room we hear a croaky voice.

MAURICE

Venus.

The place goes quiet.

(*Again, weakly.*) Venus . . .

IAN

Who the hell's Venus?

The Doctor goes in to see Maurice.

JESSIE

I am.

IAN

You are?

The Doctor comes to the door of the room.

DOCTOR
(*to Jessie*)

He wants to see you.

The Doctor smiles.

He's asked if you'll look after him.

> IAN
> (*quietly*)

Her!

Jessie stands up and goes to the door.

> JESSIE

Yes!

INT. MAURICE'S FLAT. DAY

Maurice lies there in bed. Jessie comes in.

> MAURICE

Venus. Is it really you?

> JESSIE

Yes.

The Doctor comes to the door and beckons her over. He speaks quietly to her.

> DOCTOR

He's really quite poorly. Give him two of these. He should sleep. I'll have the ambulance here in an hour or two. You understand?

> JESSIE

Yes, yes.

> DOCTOR

Can you manage?

> JESSIE

Yes.

> DOCTOR

Good.

Ian glares at her from across the room.

INT. MAURICE'S BEDROOM. DAY

Jessie sits at Maurice's bedside, where he lies, more or less asleep. She bathes his brow with a wet towel.

> JESSIE
> I'm sorry, I'm sorry! Please forgive me. Let it go, Maurice, I'll do anything. Please! I'll never be mean again!

INT. MAURICE'S FLAT. DAY

She clears up the mess in the living room. She dusts and polishes.

INT. MAURICE'S FLAT. DAY

Later. She comes into his room with a glass of water. His eyes flicker and open.

> JESSIE
> Maurice. Maurice. Can you hear me? Make a sign. (*Pause.*) Look, Maurice!

She takes off her top and shows him her breasts. She looks at him. But he is asleep.

INT. MAURICE'S KITCHEN. DAY

She is washing up, tidying, and putting things away.

INT. MAURICE'S BEDROOM. DAY

She is sitting next to him, reading slowly but carefully from his copy of the Sonnets.

> JESSIE
> 'Weary with toil, I haste me to my bed,
> The dear repose for limbs with travel tired,
> But then begins a journey in my head
> To work my mind, when's body's work's expired . . .'

He is trying to say something.

> What do you want?

He whispers in her ear. She kisses him tenderly. He smiles.

INT. MAURICE'S BEDROOM. NIGHT

She takes him along the corridor.

INT. MAURICE'S BATHROOM. DAY

In the toilet. He is sitting finishing a piss.

>   JESSIE
> Okay?

>   MAURICE
>   (*pause*)
> I don't want to go back to bed.

>   JESSIE
> They're coming to take you to the hospital now.

>   MAURICE
> But I've got you.

>   JESSIE
> Maurice . . .

>   MAURICE
> I've got a much better idea.

>   JESSIE
> Have you?

INT. MAURICE'S FRONT ROOM. DAY

*She has got him dressed: he's wearing his gardening boots, an old
overcoat, now too big for him, and an old scarf. He sits at the table
looking frail.*

>   MAURICE
> You know where the housekeeping money is, Venus.

Jessie goes to the Shakespeare jug.

EXT. MAURICE'S FLAT. DAY

They get into a cab and it departs. We see an ambulance arriving . . .

EXT. VICTORIA RAILWAY STATION. DAY

They get out of a taxi and walk onto the busy station.

EXT. VICTORIA RAILWAY STATION. DAY

As she stands at the booth buying the tickets she turns and looks worriedly at him, making sure he's okay. He looks bizarre and lost, standing there.

EXT. VICTORIA RAILWAY STATION. DAY

Maurice waits at the ticket barrier. Weakly he sits on a long trolley.

OFFICIAL
You can't sit there, mate.

MAURICE
What?

OFFICIAL
Get up, I'm moving that!

MAURICE
But you're not moving it.

OFFICIAL
I will when you get off!

Jessie comes over.

JESSIE
Hey – you! He can fucking sit where he fucking likes. You can piss off, unless you want to do something about it!

The Official stares at her before backing off. Offering him her arm, she helps Maurice up and off they go, down the platform.

MAURICE
What a fine girl you are in times of trouble, Venus.

She helps him into the train.

INT. TRAIN CARRIAGE. DAY

He looks intently out of the window. She watches him. We see the train is heading into the country.

> JESSIE
>
> What are you looking at?

> MAURICE
>
> That church. Isn't it sublime?

EXT. SEASIDE TOWN STATION. DAY

Outside the station she helps him into another taxi.

INT. BEACH RESTAURANT. DAY

A plate of oysters on the table. He watches her put it in her mouth.

> JESSIE
>
> Yum.

> MAURICE
>
> Another?

She nods.

> I knew you'd enjoy yourself.

> JESSIE
>
> Aren't you going to have one?

EXT. STREET. DAY

They come out of the restaurant.

> JESSIE
>
> I think we should go back now.

> MAURICE
>
> A little longer.

EXT. SEAFRONT. DAY

They walk on the top of the ridge, looking down at the sea.

JESSIE

Are you tired?

MAURICE

Oh yes.

JESSIE

What shall we do?

MAURICE

Carry on.

JESSIE

Yes.

They walk together.

EXT. BEACH. DAY

MAURICE

Will you take off my boot?

JESSIE

It's too cold, Maurice.

MAURICE

I know, I know. It was always bloody cold. Will you?

EXT. BEACH. DAY

They are at the shore. She helps him remove one boot and takes off his sock. He dips a toe into the water.

MAURICE

Wonderful.

EXT. BEACH. DAY

She is helping him back up the shingle bank to where there is a bench.
He sinks down.

>   MAURICE
> Now we can really talk.

>   JESSIE
> Yes.

His head lolls. He dies.

> Maurice, Maurice!

She looks around frantically. She doesn't know what to do.

EXT. BEACH. DAY

Jessie runs towards a couple walking their dog.

>   JESSIE
> Oh help, help us! Help!

EXT. BEACH. DAY

She sits there next to the dead body as the Paramedics, with their
equipment, come over the hill.

EXT. BEACH. DAY

The ambulance has arrived. As the other Paramedics carry Maurice's
covered body into the ambulance, one of the female Paramedics writes
down information.

>   PARAMEDIC
> Maurice Russell. How old?

>   JESSIE
> Old, old.

>   PARAMEDIC
> Yes, but – What is your relation to the deceased?

JESSIE

Sorry?

PARAMEDIC

Granddaughter? Niece? Friend?

Jessie looks confused.

INT. CREMATORIUM. DAY

The crematorium is packed with friends.

We watch Valerie making her way to the front.

VALERIE

He was tall, Maurice, and he was a beautiful bastard.
Handsome too, as many of you know to your cost. There
are some people, you know from the start, that if you fall
in love with them, it will ruin your life, you will feel a fool
for ever. It was foolish of me to fall so far, and I regret it,
and I can never regret it, and the children wouldn't let me
regret it, because we had as much fun as any family can.
I give thanks, to a man, to a father, to an actor, my husband,
Maurice.

INT. A LARGE HALL. DAY

*A large hall is packed with actors chucking back wine and champagne.
Jessie wanders around with a bottle, topping people up. They call her
'Darling', thank her profusely, and have no idea who she is. Everyone
is too busy talking about work, about gossip, to really care. She sees
Donald bringing Ian a drink. He is pale and upset. Two Actors are
talking about Stratford, an Actress is roaring with laughter at the end
of an anecdote, etc.*

Suddenly, Valerie is there, in front of her.

VALERIE

So it was you.

JESSIE

What?

VALERIE

His last distraction. I'm his wife. He was thinking about someone. It was you.

Jessie is embarrassed.

Don't feel awkward. Ian told me.

JESSIE

Ian still won't talk to me.

VALERIE

Why ever not?

JESSIE

He thinks I did for Maurice. The paddling and stuff.

VALERIE

The paddling was marvellous. The only way to go.

Jessie smiles. She looks around.

JESSIE

He really was a celebrity.

VALERIE

When you die everyone wants to be your friend.

JESSIE

I wish he could be here. He'd love the attention.

Valerie smiles.

VALERIE

What will you do?

JESSIE

I'm not going home. I can't go back now. And Ian won't have me in the house. I don't know.

Valerie thinks for a moment.

VALERIE

I've got somewhere you can stay. For a bit.

INT. MAURICE'S FLAT. DAY

Jessie lets herself in with a key and closes the door. She stands there, looking around at the quiet room.

INT. CAFÉ. DAY

Ian and Donald sit at their usual table reading the paper. The Waitress comes over with three coffees. Ian and Donald watch her lay Maurice's place.

WAITRESS
Where's your friend?

Ian can't speak. Instead he shows her the photograph accompanying the obituaries – a picture of Maurice as a young man.

God, he was gorgeous.

IAN
Yes he was 'gorgeous'.

He stares ahead.

Donald notices that Jessie is outside. He goes out to her and we see them talking. He leans back into the café, holding up some keys.

DONALD
She wants to return these.

IAN
Say thank you.

Donald again speaks to Jessie.

DONALD
She wants to know if you're still angry. She says she's sorry.

IAN
Tell her I'm not angry now. I just wasn't ready for someone like her.

Donald again speaks to Jessie.

DONALD
She says she'll come by tomorrow, if you want. She'll cook you some fish.

IAN

Tell her we can cook it together.

Jessie waves to him through the window and is gone.

Donald comes back in and sits down.

DONALD

How many columns did he get?

INT. ART ROOM. NIGHT

Jessie walks to the plinth and drops her dressing gown. She lies down and presents her body to the artists.

WEDDINGS AND BEHEADINGS

This piece, originally written as a 'short short' story, became a film at the end of 2006 after Amir Jamal, a documentary film-maker, suggested we could make it as a short film, in the shape of a 'video diary', with the harried protagonist talking to himself, as he prepares to go to work . . .

I have gathered the equipment together and now I am waiting for them to arrive. They will not be long; they never are.

You don't know me personally. My existence has never crossed your mind. But I would bet you've seen my work: it has been broadcast everywhere, on most of the news channels worldwide. Or at least parts of it have. You could find it on the net, right now, if you really wanted to. If you could bear to look.

Not that you'd notice my style, my artistic signature or anything like that.

I film beheadings, which are common in this war-broken city, my childhood home.

It was never my ambition, as a young man who loved cinema, to film such things. Nor was it my wish to do weddings either, though there are less of those these days. Ditto graduations and parties. My friends and I have always wanted to make real films, with living actors and dialogue and jokes and music, as we began to as students. Nothing like that is possible here.

Every day we are ageing, we feel shabby, the stories are there, waiting to be told, we're artists. But this stuff, the death work, it has taken over.

Naturally we didn't seek out this kind of employment. We were 'recommended' and we can't not do it; we can't say we're visiting relatives or working in the cutting room. They call us up with little notice at odd hours, usually at night, and minutes later they are outside with their guns. They put us in the car and cover our heads. Because there's only one of us working at a time, the thugs help with carrying the gear. But we have to do the sound as well as the picture, and load the camera and work out how to light the scene. I've asked to use an assistant, but they only offer their rough accomplices and they know nothing, they can't even wipe a lens without making a mess of it.

I know three other guys who do this work; we discuss it amongst ourselves, but we'd never talk to anyone else about it or we'd end up in front of the camera.

My closest friend filmed a beheading recently, but he's not a director, only a writer really. I wouldn't say anything, but I wouldn't trust him with a camera. He was the one who had the idea of getting calling cards made with 'Weddings and Beheadings' inscribed on them. If the power's on, we meet in his flat to watch great movies on video. He's jokey: 'Don't bury your head in the sand, my friend,' he says when we part. 'Don't go losing your head now. Chin up!'

He isn't too sure about the technical stuff, how to set up the camera, and then how to get the material through the computer and onto the internet.

It's a skill, obviously.

A couple of weeks ago he messed up badly. The cameras are good quality, they're taken from foreign journalists, but a bulb blew in the one light he was using, and he couldn't replace it. By then they had brought the victim in. My friend tried to tell the men, it's too dark, it's not going to come out and you can't do another take. But they were in a hurry, he couldn't persuade them to wait, they were already hacking through the neck and he was in such a panic he fainted. Luckily the camera was running. It came out underlit of course, what did they expect? I liked it – 'Lynchian' I called it – but they hit him around the head, and never used him again.

He was lucky. But I wonder if he's going mad. Secretly he kept copies of his beheadings and now he plays around with them on his computer, cutting and re-cutting them, and putting on music,

swing stuff, opera, jazz, comic songs. Perhaps it's the only freedom
he has.

It might surprise you, but we do get paid, they always give us
something 'for the trouble', and they even make jokes: 'You'll get
a prize for the next one. Don't you guys love prizes and statuettes
and stuff?'

But it's hellish, the long drive there with the camera and tripod
on your lap, the smell of the sack, the guns, and you wonder if
this time you might be the victim. Usually you're sick, and then
you're in the building and in the room, setting up, and you hear
things, from other rooms, that make you wonder if life on earth
is a good idea.

I know you don't want too much detail, but it's serious work
taking off someone's head if you're not a butcher, and these guys
aren't qualified, they're just enthusiastic, it's what they like to do.
To make it work on television, it helps to get a clear view of the
victim's eyes just before they cover them. At the end they hold
up the head streaming with blood and you might need to use
some hand-held here, to catch everything. It has to be framed
carefully. It wouldn't be good if you missed something. (That
means that ideally you need a quick-release tripod head, something
I have and would never lend to anyone.)

They cheer and fire off rounds while you're checking the tape
and playing it back. After, they put the body in a bag and dump
it somewhere, before they drive you to another place, where you
transfer the material to the computer and send it out.

Often I wonder what this is doing to me. I try to think of war
photographers, who, they say, use the lens to distance themselves
from the reality of suffering and death. But those guys have
elected to do that work, they believe in it. We are innocent.

One day I'd like to make a proper film, maybe beginning with a
beheading, telling the story that leads up to it. It's the living I'm
interested in, but the way things are going I'll be doing this for
a while. Sometimes I wonder if I'm going to go mad, or whether
even this escape is denied me.

I better go now. Someone is at the door.